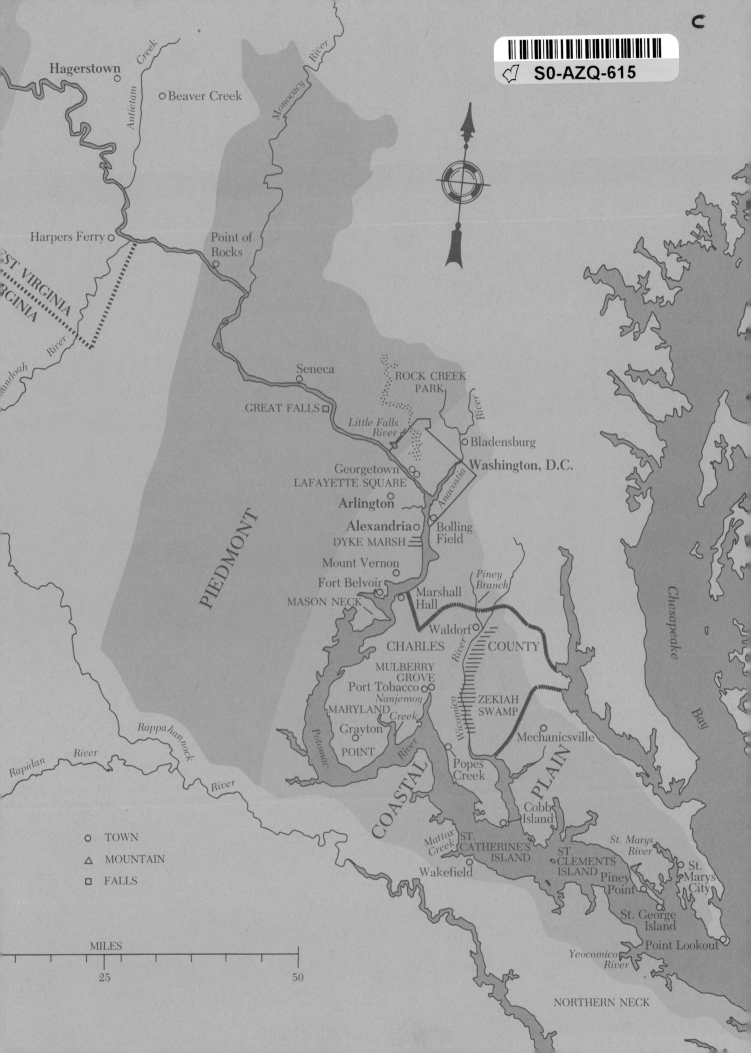

POTOMAC

ALSO BY FRANK GRAHAM, JR.

Disaster by Default: Politics and Water Pollution

Since Silent Spring

Man's Dominion: The Story of Conservation in America

Where the Place Called Morning Lies

Gulls: A Social History

POTOMAC

The Nation's River

by Frank Graham, Jr.

Photographs by Edward Schell

J.B. LIPPINCOTT COMPANY
Philadelphia & New York

Printed in the United States of America

U.S. Library of Congress Cataloging in Publication Data

Graham, Frank, birth date
   Potomac: the nation's river.

   Bibliography: p.
   1. Potomac Valley—History.   I.   Schell, Edward.
II.   Title.
F187.P8G7   975.2   75-40164
ISBN-0-397-01139-3

*To those who have devoted their energies and talents
to bringing about the preservation of the Potomac
and its designation as the Potomac National River*

CONTENTS

Photographs and captions by Edward Schell follow pages 24, 49, 67, 87, and 109.

ACKNOWLEDGMENTS

Like everyone else who is concerned about the Potomac, we owe a debt of gratitude to Congressman Gilbert Gude of Maryland for his long and imaginative struggle on behalf of the river's protection.

The photographer would like to thank Eliot Porter for the encouragement given him at a crucial moment, while the author would like to thank Shirley A. Briggs of the Rachel Carson Trust for the Living Environment for the many courtesies she extended during his research.

Others who helped with advice include the rangers and naturalists of the Monongahela National Forest, Shenandoah National Park, Harpers Ferry National Historical Park, C & O National Historical Park, and Mount Vernon. Important help was given by Merle McManigle of the Gauley Ranger District, Chandler S. Robbins of the U.S. Fish and Wildlife Service, and Agnes and Hugh Crandall and S. Preston Smith of the National Park Service at Shenandoah and Harpers Ferry.

Finally, we thank our wives, Ada and Barbara, for their very real contributions to the inception and preparation of this book.

Frank Graham, Jr.
Edward Schell

PART I

TIDEWATER

"Then on the 3 of March, 1634, we came into Chesapeake baye, at the mouth of the Potomecke," wrote Father Andrew White, S.J., in his *Brief Relation*. "This is the sweetest and greatest river I have seene, so that the Thames in England is but a little finger to it."

Father White, who was in the company of twenty gentlemen and three hundred laborers aboard two venturesome ships, the *Ark* and the *Dove*, saw the Potomac River from the deck of the *Ark* as no one will ever see it again. The company had come to settle Lord Baltimore's Terre Mariae, or Maryland, on the north side of the Potomac where the St. Marys River joins it. To the Jesuit's curious gaze the elevated shore presented a sheer façade, cliffs rising sometimes to a hundred feet above the river, crowned by the unbroken forest. The land must have seemed indomitable, unrelieved by clearings that might have offered the newcomers a few reassuring footholds. The party's first landing was on St. Clements Island, "solid firme ground," said Father White, "with great variety of woode, not choaked up with undershrubs, but commonly so farre distant from each other as a coach and fower horses may travale without molestation."

Father White planted a cross in the "solid firme ground," but it was the river that proved to be the more durable. The forest on the mainland was swept away by the settlers, the island by the ceaseless swirl of the river; the 400 acres of land which Father White ascribed to St. Clements Island has been eroded to a mere 40 acres today, while the state of Maryland tries to save the remnant. Even Father White's cross has disappeared. (A huge concrete commemorative cross was raised on the island in 1934, the three hundredth anniversary of the landing.)

Early settlers of the tidewater country must have stared apprehensively up into the maw of the river as it moved sluggishly toward them, its flow a precipitate of the massed white clouds that hung over the unknown forests of the interior. To most of those people the Potomac's upper reaches were as great a mystery as the far side of the moon. By 1634 a few traders from the Virginia colony had already ventured into the upper Potomac Valley, but despite Father White's reference to coaches and horses it would be a long time before travel or transportation in that direction by land was practical for any but the hardiest. Even the new communities were linked to each other, as they were to the mother country, by water. And so the river that slid past them loomed large in their minds.

Shortly the newcomers set out to bridle the exuberant wilderness that was a source of their anxiety. With shot and shell they altered the composition of its native life, human and otherwise. They altered the aspect of the land itself. And later other men changed the composition of the river's flow, taking from it the almost incredible richness of fish that sustained the colonists and putting back, all too often, the wastes from their towns, their farms, and their mines. The river continued to rip away some of the land, as it did at St. Clements Island, though elsewhere it deposited the loads of silt and muck washed into it from mismanaged farms and forests, and thus filled up once-productive harbors, marshes, and inlets. But from the standpoint of the geographer and the geologist, the river and the land it drains remain very much in their outlines what they were when Father White saw them.

The Potomac that the settlers first saw was in fact the river's estuary. This is its lower reaches, its tidal portion, where the fresh water drained from the inland country meets and mingles with the salt water creeping up the river's mouth from the sea. The Potomac's estuary is nearly a hundred miles long, a broad, sluggish mass of brackish water moving over the mud and silt carried downstream and deposited by the river itself after it has plunged over the falls above what is now the city of Washington. The river has left behind the steep slopes of the mountains, its pace adjusted here by the flattened terrain of the coastal plain that forms the riverbed and the surrounding tidewater country.

Like every estuary, the Potomac's is a region of combating forces. As the cold water from highland streams collides with the salt water pulsing upstream, it forms a mixture that varies in quality from season to season and even from hour to hour. Depending on the strength of the river's flow (a tumultuous surge during wet springs, a diminished volume in dry summers) or on the state of the tide, the estuary's salinity rises and falls. Mud and sediments may be stirred up in the watery clash, restricting the amount of light that pours through to living things below. The water's temperature fluctuates in response to the mixture's composition as well as to the ambient climate.

One ecologist has determined that an estuary is twenty times more productive than the open sea. In these large inlets from the sea, often bordered by rich stretches of salt marsh, creatures of all kinds start their lives and are nurtured to maturity. Both the river and the sea contribute nutrients to the teeming nursery. The estuary, pulsing with seawater pumped from the Atlantic, rises and falls, flooding the bordering marshes and, as the tide ebbs, draining away additional nutrients from their rich ooze. Oysters are among the many creatures fitted to survive in the changing conditions of the estuary. Although they spend the early days of their lives among the plankton, drifting helplessly on the water's surface, these mollusks soon settle to the bottom, find a place in the mud, and become sessile. They feed by straining nutrients from the water that flows over them.

Many other animals spend parts or all of their lives living on the estuary's bounty. Shad swim in from the sea to spawn. Ospreys and terns fly over the surface, diving to capture fish. Long-legged herons stalk the marshes and shallows in search of small aquatic animals. Bald eagles and gulls scavenge the shore.

Any colonists who expected to find the shores of the Potomac paved with gold must have soon been diverted by the richness of living things they found there. This is an opulent land, and the colonists' early accounts of it are vibrant with descriptions of the birds, beasts, and fishes they marveled at and quickly put to use. In his *Generall Historie of Virginia*, Captain John Smith wrote of the rivers along the coast.

> The fourth river is called Potawomecke, 6 or 7 myles in breadth. It is navigable 140 myles and fed as the rest with many sweet rivers and springs, which fall from the bordering hills. These hills many of them are planted, and yield no less plentie and varietie of fruit, than the river exceedeth with abundance of fish.

Explorers from the colony Sir Walter Raleigh had planted on Roanoke Island in 1584 probably discovered the "Potawomecke" as they sailed up Chesapeake Bay in search of that long-sought Northwest Passage to the Orient. Smith, the copiously whiskered, swashbuckling soldier of fortune ("Brass without, Golde within," as he described himself), had seen a great deal of the world since he had set out on his own at the age of sixteen. He had recorded many deeds of derring-do, some of them probably figments of his robust imagination. But even he was impressed when he and his fourteen-man crew spied the mouth of the broad river as they probed Chesapeake Bay's western shore in their open barge on June 16, 1608. The fish, he wrote, were "lying so thicke with their heads above the water" that his crew tried to scoop them up with frying pans. As Smith explored the river and reached Little Falls above the present site of the District of Columbia (mistaking Capitol Hill and the heights of Arlington for "mountains"), he probably saw the huge sturgeon which then flourished in the Potomac. These great, primitive, bottom-dwelling monsters (Hiawatha's Misha-Nahma, "King of Fishes"), heavily armored and said to live sometimes for a century, came up the river to spawn. Their roe, prized around the world as caviar, caused them to be pursued ruthlessly, until they all but disappeared from the river.

The Indians on the Virginia shore—chiefly the Algonkian tribes then ruled in a confederacy by the powerful chief Powhatan—used the living things around them with skill and shrewdness. An early writer noted that they had distinct names for eighty-six kinds of fowl and thirty-six kinds of beasts. They taught the colonists to fish with traps and spears; having no iron or steel, some Indians of the region used the sharp tails of horseshoe crabs to tip their spears. When Lord Baltimore's settlers landed in Maryland, they found the Indians in the process of abandoning the productive fields behind the dense forest that had veiled them from the river, so the settlers gratefully took over the fields as their own. They even took the Indians' name for the area around what is now Washington—Potawomecke, or "trading place"—and applied it to the river.

As the decades passed, the colonists exceeded the Indians in the thoroughness—one might almost say the *finality*—with which they harvested the land's bounty. Abundant in John Smith's time was the heath hen (an eastern race of the prairie chicken), which the new Americans finally shot to extinction as they did the passenger pigeon, common in Virginia, which even as late as Audubon's time (1785–1851) darkened the sky with its numbers in flight. Beavers disappeared from the region under the white traders' insatiable demand for pelts.

The colonists, as every schoolboy knows, took up the Indians' art of cultivating maize, or corn, and quickly made use of the vast forests around them. Huge oaks and walnuts (the latter sometimes soaring eighty feet before the first limbs grew out from the trunk) were among the most conspicuous trees. The colonists cut oaks for timber and later devastated the stands of walnut. They built weirs and fish traps from the willows; chests, boxes, ceilings, and virginals from the cedars; and ships' masts from the "fir" (perhaps the hemlock). In southern Maryland they felled the towering cypresses, which now survive for the most part only as boards in old houses.

But though the colonists' resource-based livelihood stripped the land of much of its variety, they could not blot out its beauty. That persisted, and remains to this day. It was a good land, and colonists came crowding in. Leonard Calvert, Lord Baltimore's brother, led the party that proceeded from St. Clements Island to the northern shore of the Potomac and founded Maryland in 1634. Under a huge mulberry tree, Calvert bargained with the Piscataway Indians for part of the land around a village that was soon to be abandoned. For a collection of cloth, rakes, and axes, the colonists received permission to take over the village and the neighboring countryside after the

next harvest, and the village became the first town in the new colony, St.
Marys. A nineteenth-century writer, quoted by Robert E. T. Pogue in his
Old Maryland Landmarks, commemorated the transaction and the tree:

> Over these ruins a storm-shaken and magnificent mulberry, aboriginal and contemporary with the settlement of this province, yet rears its shattered and topless trunk, and daily distils upon the sacred relics at its foot, the dews of heaven—an august and brave mourner to the departed companions of its prime.

The mulberry has gone, replaced by a monument to Calvert.

Across the river an extraordinary civilization was taking shape late in the seventeenth century. At first the wealth there, as in many other parts of North America, was founded on the beaver. The early colonists not involved in securing rich furs from the interior were for the most part tied to extracting survival rations from the land and nearby waters. There were the crops the Indians taught them to raise—corn, beans, squash, and pumpkins—and the various game and seafood that were free for the taking. Wild turkeys, for example, were still abundant in the forests. Old Ben Franklin had a point when he scorned that scavenger, the bald eagle, as a "bad moral character" unfit to serve for a national emblem and campaigned instead for the turkey; like Al Capp's shmoo, the turkey fatuously offered up its toothsome body for others' delectation, thus helping to sustain the colonists through those difficult early days. (Its few surviving descendants, fortunately, have eschewed foolishness to become as wary as foxes.)

By the 1630s tobacco was already ascendant among the commercial products of the tidewater country. Tobacco was also a gift from the Indians, their *apooke*. The colonists were quick to grasp the potential value of this plant which is native to the new world. Although the leaf of the tidewater variety was small, it flourished in those sandy loams and other marine deposits, and the colonists imported larger-leaved plants from the West Indies. Proper selection produced further improvements. Europe opened its arms wide to the delights of this miracle weed, and tobacco (jotted *tob⁰* in thousands of contemporary ledgers and bills of lading) became king of the tidewater country as, to the south and the north of it, cotton and cod ruled their own domains.

The tobacco leaves were cured in little barns and sheds. They were bargained for, packed in hogsheads, and loaded aboard ships in the ports that sprang up in harbors and inlets all along the lower Potomac. From there, hardy seamen set forth with the precious cargo to match their skills against the hazards of ponderous seas. The sale of the cured leaves in London brought cash to the Potomac colonies.

Tobacco proved to be a tyrannical master. Prices fluctuated greatly and, as every farmer knows, beyond the grower's control; London dealers and their agents, as well as the whims of the buying public, established the amounts paid for the harvests.

Port Tobacco was perhaps typical of those early river towns in the sultry lowlands. Like many of them, it rose from the ruins of an Indian settlement. Potapaco, the Piscataways had called it, years before the white man came, and the name was grasped and altered only slightly to fit its new circumstances. Port Tobacco became the center of population in Maryland, and tobacco itself the currency of the region.

A ferry across the Potomac linked Port Tobacco with the Virginia shore. The two colonies were united then in their interests, not only in the commerce that dominated their lives but also in the ugly institution that supported it—slavery. Slaves worked the tobacco fields and staffed the huge plantations that were put together by the tobacco gentry. Indeed, it has been said that Harriet Beecher Stowe took the idea for *Uncle Tom's Cabin* from an account of the hardships of a slave who had escaped to Canada from tidewater Maryland's Charles County.

Yet out of this slave society grew some of the great names in American history. Near Port Tobacco rose Mulberry Grove, the home of that John Hanson who was elected our "first President" by the Continental Congress in 1781. Mulberry trees throve there, but the silkworms that were to be the basis of a local silk industry did not. Across the river the peninsula called the Northern Neck, which lies between the Potomac and the Rappahannock rivers, was granted in 1688 by King James II to Lord Culpeper. This tract, which became the largest of the tidewater holdings, passed by inheritance to Lord Fairfax. There, along the Potomac, the Fairfax family built its splendid manor, Belvoir. (It is the site of Fort Belvoir today.)

Other homes that were to become famous were built on the Northern Neck. In 1657 the merchant ship *Seahorse of London* arrived at Mattox Creek to pick up a cargo of tobacco. Before the vessel could leave, however, it sank in a sudden storm. Its second officer, John Washington, decided to stay in Virginia, where he married a daughter of Colonel Nathaniel Pope, received a plantation as a wedding gift from his father-in-law, and founded the Virginia family that was to produce the "Father" of the new nation. James Monroe, James Madison, George Mason, John Marshall, and Robert E. Lee were other men descended from early settlers who built their homes on Northern Neck. The great plantations of a thousand acres or more, with their slaves, their forests, their vegetable gardens, and their livestock, became self-sufficient communities.

Mount Vernon, if not the grandest of those plantations, is surely the most famous. When George Washington inherited the property from his elder half-brother, Lawrence, in 1752 the house was an unimposing little building, but it shared with its more elegant neighbors a magnificent prospect over the Potomac. Seven years later the building was enlarged from one and a half to two and a half stories as a part of the preparations for Washington's marriage. He also made plans to build additions at each end of the house, though they were not carried out until after the Revolution. Around the evolving mansion rose the various gardens and outbuildings needed to sustain an eighteenth-century plantation.

Washington himself has receded through the years so that he is something of a legend in the common imagination, an aloof avatar of probity outfitted in wigs and wooden teeth. (He wore neither, the fashion of wigs for men having passed before the Revolution, while his own teeth, as they disappeared, were replaced by false ones of ivory or porcelain, or perhaps even by human teeth, bought from the poor as was customary at the time.) But his plantation, rescued and restored on five hundred acres by the Mount Vernon Ladies Association, has come down to us through the mists of time as a vivid presence, a blend of charming interiors and fragrant, color-splashed grounds.

For many of the colonists there was an abiding wonder and delight in the rich natural treasure chest of the New World. Despite the hardships, Virginia seemed a new Eden, alive with marvelous plants and animals. In his *History and Present State of Virginia*, published in 1705, Robert Beverly described the world in which he and his fellow Virginians lived:

> Their Ears are Serenaded with the perpetual murmur of Brooks, and the thorow-base which the Wind plays, when it wantons through the Trees; the merry Birds, too, join their pleasing Notes to this rural Consort, especially the Mock-Birds, who love Society so well, that whenever they see Mankind, they will perch upon a Twigg very near them, and sing the sweetest wild Airs in the World. . . . Their Taste is regaled with the most delicious Fruits, which, without Art, they have in great variety and perfection. And then their smell is refreshed with an eternal fragrancy of Flowers and Sweets, with which Nature perfumes and adorns the Woods almost the whole year round.

There were many serpents, real or imagined, in this Eden too. The forest had its menacing aspect. "Virginia Rangers" roamed the backcountry to eliminate wolves, Indians, and other threats to society's commerce and well-being. As we now realize to our chagrin, these public defenders often performed their duties only too well.

But this was a society that consumed more than wolves and Indians. The beavers had retreated to remote regions of the interior. Deer, turkeys, and other game began to disappear. Great numbers of waterfowl were shot; it is said that one of the most persistent sources of grumbling among the slaves was the steady diet of canvasback ducks they were given. (The canvasback now is considered the duck of the gourmet!)

More damaging still was the depletion of the soil, an evil of long duration. It began when the first settlers felled and burned the forests to clear the land for their farms and plantations. Constant erosion deprived the land of its topsoil. The soil entered streams and rivers and finally began to silt up the harbors. Once-thriving ports that had handled oceangoing craft soon became shallow inlets, then marshes, and finally dry land. Today Port Tobacco is an inland town, separated from the deep water that once sustained it by hundreds of yards of earth swept there by the river from hillsides elsewhere in the region. Blackbirds fly over marshes where ducks and geese once paddled.

Tobacco was hard on the land. Later agriculturists have referred to tobacco planters as "mining" the soil. That is an accurate description, for the plants soon extracted all nourishing minerals from the soil and left it exhausted. The planters used neither fertilizers nor crop rotation; theirs was a true "monoculture." One of the reasons that plantations grew so large was that, after a few years, the soil became useless for growing anything at all, and the planters had to abandon it and move on to another plot.

The tobacco society was doomed. Smaller planters moved west, leaving tobacco to their betters, and started a new life raising grains and livestock in the rich limestone lands of the high valleys. Thomas Jefferson, surveying his fading holdings, observed that tobacco "was productive of infinite wretchedness," while a few years after George Washington's death his plantation was described as a "perfect agricultural ruin."

By the close of the eighteenth century, the golden years were past in the tidewater tobacco culture. More and more the countryside became a scatter of relict farms, abandoned to catbrier and silence. Using new agricultural methods, however, some of the planters persisted, wringing a hard living from their thin soils. They clung to their traditions, and in Maryland, although the Baltimore industrialists helped keep the state in the Union during the Civil War, the planters of its southernmost counties actively sympathized with the Confederacy.

Colonel Lafayette C. Baker of the United States Secret Service (and the man who organized the capture of John Wilkes Booth after Lincoln's assassination) has left us an unflattering picture of Port Tobacco during the war:

> If any place in the world is utterly given over to depravity, it is Port Tobacco. Before the war, Port Tobacco was the seat of a tobacco aristocracy and a haunt of negro traders. It passed very naturally into a rebel post for blockade runners and a rebel postoffice general. Gambling, corner fighting, and shooting matches were its lyceum education. . . . The Courthouse of Port Tobacco is the most superfluous house in the place, except for the church.

An observer in our own time, Calvert R. Posey, has brought the picture up to date in his *Ecological History of Charles County, Maryland*:

> The economy of the country was to a large degree tied up in slave labor. Thus, with the freeing of the slaves the planters of Charles County faced ruin. Tobacco had ruined the land, slavery had ruined the people, and now the very basis of land tenure was being taken away; much of the land . . . was abandoned to return to forest.

Although weakened, tobacco still holds its grip on the region and keeps its rural people poor. Tourists may yet attend tobacco auctions in towns such as La Plata, and a drive through the wooded countryside reveals a variety of barns, some of them two hundred years old, where tobacco was and still is cured. The hand-hewn white pine in those barns has almost disappeared in the wild, but the old buildings have stood up to the tidewater hurricanes better than the high-roofed ones of this century.

With tobacco's decline, the rich estuary took on an even greater importance. In this vast natural mixing bowl, where the nourishing seawater slides in under the lighter freshets coming from the mountains inland, the splendid nursery for both shellfish and finfish remains. George Washington knew these fisheries. In August 1768 his schooner ran aground on one of the oyster bars jutting into the Potomac while he was seining for sheepshead near Morgantown. He was, Washington noted in his diary, "hauling seine upon the bar off Cedar Point but catched none." Today the sheepshead, like so much else of that time, are gone from the Potomac.

But the estuary was worth fighting over, and men did. A curious political aspect of this river which flows for so much of its maturity between the shores of Maryland and Virginia is that it is not shared by the two states equally. By right of the old royal grants, Maryland holds title to the river all the way across to the high-water mark on the Virginia shore. Through the years watermen from both states have squabbled over fishing rights in the river, especially over the lush beds of oysters and soft-shell clams. Heads were sometimes broken and blood flowed, but the profits were considerable. To the oysters' sweetness was added the enticement provided by the local people's belief that their flesh was a potent sex stimulant. "Eat oysters, love longer," remains an incomparable advertising slogan!

If the estuary's natural treasures established it as a center of the fishing industry, they were slower to make it a fashionable resort. During the sultry summer months the wealthy people of Washington and the surrounding area in the late nineteenth century usually fled to Saratoga, Cape May, and other distant gathering places then in fashion. Their less-fortunate brethren made do with the Potomac's lower reaches, especially on short excursions. Writing in *Forest and Stream* in 1873, Charles A. Pilsbury mentioned some of the resorts close to Washington and continued, "Farther down the river are Glymont and Marshall Hall, accessible by excursion boats and resorted to by picnic parties and yachting parties. Here rum and riot sometimes prevail, but there are 'select excursions' which provide their own champagne, and indulge in gentlemanly intoxication by moonlight or otherwise."

But more often than not it was the abundant seafood—crabs, oysters, and finfish—that proved the lure. At Piney Point, where the estuary broadens to five miles, a resort grew up which was sometimes called "the Southern Long Branch." Shad bakes were popular there, as well as bathing. "The bottom is hard and sandy," Pilsbury tells us, "but as one occasionally encounters an oyster shell it is advisable to wear bathing shoes."

During the War of 1812 patriotic watermen along the estuary were said to have confused the British Navy by moving around the navigation aids and stranding the ships on the oyster bars. In the years since then the people of the Potomac have often outfoxed themselves. By clearing the forests whose roots once held the rainwater on the hillsides upstream, they have set loose floods of fresh water that overwhelm the saline-loving oysters and push them gradually back toward the Potomac's mouth. In our time the productive oyster beds extend upstream only to about the area of Port Tobacco, twenty miles below their deepest penetration fifty years ago.

In 1972 Hurricane Agnes, abetted by man's accumulated wastes, wrought even greater destruction among the shellfish of the Potomac and Chesapeake Bay. The resultant floods, carrying sewage and chemicals, forced saline water out of the river and smothered or contaminated many of the bottom-dwelling organisms. The authorities were forced to close the polluted shellfish beds, and economic hardship spread throughout the region.

"After the hurricane, almost all the fish we examined had clam siphons in their stomachs," a local biologist said. "Why so many? Well, maybe the clams pushed their siphons higher out of the mud to get at the kind of water they needed, and the movement attracted the fish."

The tidewater region remains rewarding to those men and women to whom a landscape is barren without a variety of birdlife. A bird-watching fisherman speaks without rancor of seeing the great blue herons at night, perched on the stakes that hold his nets in the river at Point Lookout, eating the herring and menhaden which he sells as bait to crabbers. Irston R. Barnes, the prominent conservationist, says he watched in astonishment as a little blue-gray gnatcatcher built its nest, using strips of cedar bark and "cobweb" from a cankerworm's nest, in only three hours. A teacher reports taking her class at evening into the loblolly pine forest to listen to the chuck-will's-widow, that whippoorwill with a Southern accent. And near St. George Island, a party out for an early spring picnic takes pleasure in watching an osprey, the magnificent fish hawk, fly past, carrying in its talons a stout twig to repair its nest on an artificial nesting platform in the river. Until very recently Coast Guardsmen had pulled down all osprey nests built on buoys and other navigation aids, throwing even eggs and young birds into the water; now, after public protest, inviting nesting platforms are often set up next to navigation aids and are readily accepted by the big birds.

Other birds have not been so fortunate in the area. The bald eagle, as in so many other places, is declining along the Potomac, its favored nesting sites bulldozed by developers and its dull white eggs rendered sterile by long-lasting chemical pesticides in the environment. According to a recent census only twenty active bald-eagle nests remain along the entire river, producing ten eaglets in Maryland and two in Virginia. The heath hen, of course, is gone, as is the passenger pigeon, the last confirmed sightings in the wild having taken place before the end of the nineteenth century.

It is of something more than passing interest that the last unconfirmed sighting of passenger pigeons that may have some validity was made in the Virginia countryside by a President of the United States. While he was in office, Theodore Roosevelt built a house near Charlottesville, spending on it, observers of the recent White House scene may be interested to hear, less than five hundred dollars. On May 18, 1907, Roosevelt saw what he later insisted was a flock of a dozen "wild pigeons," a common name for passenger pigeons. Although he was an enthusiastic, if not expert, bird watcher and was familiar with the similar mourning dove, most of his scientific friends remained skeptical. Roosevelt, hardly a man to lose faith in himself, persisted until he had found a foreman on a nearby estate who said that he had seen wild pigeons too. The President promptly revealed the news in a magazine article. Subsequently, other ornithologists admitted the possibility that he had seen passenger pigeons, and though no one will ever be able to prove it one way or another, it remains an agreeable speculation.

Roosevelt, though a New Yorker, came to love the tidewater country, both for its wild things and the bright halo of its history. That love shines through a letter he wrote to his children after he and Mrs. Roosevelt had visited George Washington's birthplace, Wakefield, at Pope's Creek, Virginia, on an April morning:

> Every vestige of the house is destroyed, but a curious and rather pathetic thing is that, although it must be a hundred years since the place was deserted, there are still multitudes of flowers which must have come from those in the old garden. There are iris and narcissus and a little blue flower, with a neat, prim, clean smell that makes one feel as if it ought to be put with lavender into chests of fresh old linen. The narcissus in particular was growing around everywhere, together with real wild flowers like the painted columbine and star of bethlehem. It was on a lovely spot on a headland overlooking a broad inlet from the Potomac. There was also the old graveyard or grave plot in which were the grave-stones of Washington's father and mother and grandmother. All pretty nearly ruined. It was lovely warm weather and Mother and I enjoyed our walk through the funny lonely old country. Mockingbirds, meadow-larks, Carolina wrens, cardinals and field sparrows were singing cheer-fully.

Roosevelt would be pleased to know that the site was restored early in the 1930s and is now administered as a national monument by the National Park Service.

In small numbers, the seaside sparrow breeds in the brackish marshes of the Potomac estuary. Here in a bayberry shrub one defends his territory.

The New Year's evening sun silhouettes Tom Courtney's boat. Tom, a waterman, uses his boats to count the huge concentrations of sea ducks between Point Lookout and the mouth of the Yeocomico River for the annual Christmas bird count of the Southern Maryland Audubon Society.

Sanderlings feed on the minutiae turned loose by the retreating surf. They are found along Chesapeake Bay and on the river near Point Lookout, a few in spring and more in fall migrations.

Marshes along the tidewater Potomac shores are among the most important natural resources in the nation. In reality a part of the Chesapeake wetlands, they serve as a nursery for many important food and sport fish found on the continental shelf. This marsh is near St. Marys City, Maryland.

Great cormorants roost on channel markers near the bridge from Piney Point to St. George Island. The recent discovery of this wintering colony on the Potomac marks the southernmost wintering grounds in North America and is the only known colony inland from the ocean.

Snowy and great egrets breed in several heronries along the lower reaches of the Potomac, notably at St. Catherine's Island near the mouth of the Wicomico River. Here they nest in mixed colonies with black-crowned night herons, little blue herons, and an occasional Louisiana heron.

A bullhead lily looks up from Zekiah Swamp in Charles County, Maryland.
The Smithsonian Institution has identified this freshwater wetland as most
eligible for conservation action in the state of Maryland.

Laughing gulls, so-called because of their raucous cry, are common in the
tidal areas between Point Lookout and Washington during the breeding
season. This group was attracted to the spot by a school of minnows. Now
they are resting after a frenzied chase for food.

A horse barn near Mechanicsville, Maryland, shows a roofline typical of early tide-water Potomac architecture. This style was common in both homes and barns.

George Washington viewed the changing seasons of the Potomac from this vantage point at Mount Vernon. As a naturalist of some skill, he must have been delighted by the blossoming of the red-bud trees above the river. The redbud flower marks the advent of spring in the tidewater region.

The scene is never the same. One hundred years ago a forest stood here, on St. George Island. But time and wind and wave have worked their will. All that remains are a few stumps as the river claims the land. One hundred years from now even these will be gone and only the river will remain.

A great blue heron returns to its nest along Nanjemoy Creek (near Grayton, Maryland.) This heronry of about two hundred nests has been identified by the Department of Interior, the Maryland Department of Natural Resources, Nature Conservancy, and the Smithsonian Institution as an important natural resource. In spite of this it was recently damaged by lumbering operations.

Looking toward Mount Vernon, the rippled reflections of the setting sun provide a background for bulrushes at Marshall Hall. Near this spot the greater prairie chicken was last recorded before its extinction in the state of Maryland.

Salt-marsh reed grass is a lovely native of the tidewater Potomac. These strong yet graceful heads rise above the marsh at Wakefield, Washington's birthplace.

Monroe Lake on Piney Branch near Waldorf,
Maryland, supported a colony of beavers
within thirteen "crow miles" of Washington.
Today they are gone, victims of the ever-
expanding suburbs. Already the surveyors
have cut their lines for tomorrow's sub-
division. Where did the beavers go?

Like a vast expanse of mother-of-pearl, the
Potomac reflects the subtle colors of the late
afternoon. Bald eagles and ospreys still vie
with each other for the once plentiful fish at
this spot near Maryland Point.

PART II

THE CITY

Occasionally there is that gifted naturalist or explorer who, in the accounts of his travels, causes the remote places of the earth to glow with the aura of his own unique perceptions. When idling with such a book we yearn for those places, though the voyage may be ever beyond our hopes—lands that we shall never see. Burton and Stanley created Africa for millions of readers. Bates and Humboldt set others dreaming of Amazon streams where jaguars coughed by night; Wallace illuminated the Malay archipelago, Hudson the Pampas, and Doughty the Arabian Desert. Sometimes the wildness is revealed closer to our doorstep. John Muir shone his light on the "wilderness temples" of the Sierra, and Henry Beston shone his on the face of the sea off the Great Beach at Cape Cod, while Henry Thoreau ennobled the Maine Woods, and even little Walden Pond, with his special way of seeing.

It was not until 1947 that any naturalist did the same for a great modern city, and the city was, appropriately, Washington. That was the year that Louis J. Halle published his book *Spring in Washington*, which was an account of his heady adventure two years before when he "undertook to be monitor of the Washington seasons." Neither Burton, Humboldt, Bates, nor Wallace ever saw sights more wonderful than did Halle, a government employee, as he bicycled around Washington and its environs "when the government was not looking." He listened to the first "spring" song of the cardinal as it perched on a dead tree in a city street before the end of January. He saw forsythia burst into golden bloom on the fourth of March; on the same day he stalked that needle-nosed "timberdoodle" of the north woods, the woodcock, through the underbrush along the Potomac and listened to a meadowlark below Mount Vernon. He watched swans and herons (apparently otherwise unnoticed by the city's residents) flying over the Capitol and saw the buds of elms and willows unfold all over town (cherries are not the only trees that bloom in Washington). He saw Dyke Marsh reveal its teeming life as spring progressed. And he was present at that greatest miracle of all, the pageant of the migrating legions of varicolored wood warblers which descended on the city and then disappeared again on their passage from the tropics to their breeding grounds in the north.

"The flowering of the Japanese cherry trees," Halle commented, "is not so wonderful as the wave of warblers that passes through the countryside in mid-May, remaining sometimes only a day."

In this little classic, Halle made manifest to the people of Washington that, whereas other great cities grudgingly admit bits and pieces of the natural world within their hostile walls, the nation's capital deserved longer than most its reputation as "the city in the woods." In his original design, the architect Pierre Charles L'Enfant saw the federal city built around the greensward of the Mall, its tree-lined avenues radiating out toward the river and the wooded places inland. Rock Creek Park, until lesser city planners and the highway builders sank their insensitive fingers into it, was one of the most extraordinary urban parks in the world. Theodore Roosevelt found Rock Creek "as wild as a stream in the White Mountains," and until after World War II it kept this character as it flowed through the city into the Potomac. In one of the memorable passages of his book, Halle describes how he discovered a pair of veeries, thrushes which had not been known to breed south of central New Jersey, except in the mountains, nesting in a wooded thicket in Rock Creek Park. He was led to them, of course, by their song, which he describes as not comparable to that of any other bird.

> This voice is merely uncanny and unearthly [Halle wrote]. It has a soft, reedy double tone, such as might conceivably be produced by a violinist drawing his bow across two strings at once; but no mechanical instrument could produce such thin, resonant chords. It has also a windy quality, and perhaps one could give an idea of it by comparing it to the sound produced by blowing across the top of a bottle. The overtone, the resonance, as if the bird carried its own echo within itself, might make one think that the song was actually issuing from inside a bottle. It is a soft, tremulous, utterly ethereal sound, swirling downward and ending, swirling downward and ending again. Heard in the gloom of twilight, back and forth across the marshes, it gives the impression that this is no bird at all but some spirit not to be discovered.

It was passages such as this that set Northerners yearning for spring in Washington as they might have envied Bates his Amazon or Wallace his Java. In a curious harbinger of this passage, an earlier naturalist in Washington, John Burroughs, wrote in *Wake Robin* of hearing "the veery thrush" in the trees near the White House during the 1860s, "and one April morning about six o'clock he came and blew his soft mellow flute in a pear tree in my garden." The veery apparently does not sing until it reaches its nesting grounds, so it is possible that veeries once nested in Washington, then simply passed over the city in the years between the Civil War and World War II.

At any rate, it is not likely that Burroughs, the revered "John o' Birds," was mistaken about the bird's identity. As a native of New York State, he was familiar with the mating songs of all the thrushes of that area and, indeed, suggested to his great friend Walt Whitman the device of using the hermit thrush, "the gray-brown bird," to lament the murdered Lincoln in "When Lilacs Last in the Dooryard Bloom'd."

The Founding Fathers knew what they were about when they selected this place as a fitting capital for the new nation. It lies near the head of the estuary, below Great Falls where the Potomac drops from the hard rocks of the piedmont plateau to the soft sand, gravel, and clay of the coastal plain, or tidewater country. This is the "fall line," a prominent geologic and historic feature of the Middle Atlantic and Southeastern states. It marks the limit of navigation upstream for all rivers of the region, from Georgia to New York. Here, at the foot of the falls, settlements sprang up, serving as transshipment points for produce and goods going up or down the rivers and, on some of them (though not the Potomac), becoming the site of hydroelectric stations that fueled local heavy industries. Macon, Augusta, Columbia, Raleigh, Richmond, Baltimore, Wilmington, Philadelphia, and Trenton owe their existence and importance to the fall line. Before the District of Columbia was conceived, Georgetown and Alexandria grew up during colonial times on opposite banks of the Potomac just below the Great Falls, where the river makes its abrupt drop to the coastal plain. Sailing ships arrived there to unload their cargoes from Europe, a hundred miles above the Potomac's mouth.

At this point the federal government carved sixty-four square miles from Maryland and thirty-two square miles from Virginia, including the city of Alexandria, to create the District of Columbia. In 1846, by an Act of Congress, Virginia's portion retroceded to that state because the federal city was growing so slowly.

And, indeed, for a long time the capital was not much of a city. L'Enfant's vision seemed to fade in the mosquitoes and mud of the sultry tidewater country, and it was fortunate for early Presidents such as Washington and Jefferson that they were naturalists and so the struggling city was not a completely dismal spectacle to them. Even John Quincy Adams took his pleasure where he could find it, slipping away from the White House occasionally for a cooling dip in the broad Potomac. John Burroughs came to work at the Treasury Department in 1863 and celebrated Washington not for its urban qualities but for the extensive wilderness and the wild things he found within its borders. He described those things in loving detail, as in the following note written on March 4, 1865, a few hours after he had attended Lincoln's second inauguration:

The afternoon was very clear and warm—real vernal sunshine at last, though the wind roared like a lion over the woods. It seemed novel enough to find within two miles of the White House a simple woodsman chopping away as if no President was being inaugurated. . . . This day, for the first time, I heard the song of the Canada sparrow [the white-throated sparrow], a soft, sweet note, almost running into a warble. Saw a small, black, velvety butterfly with a yellow border to its wings. Under a warm bank found two flowers of the houstonia in bloom. Saw frogs' spawn near Piny Branch, and heard the hyla.

But "John o' Birds" could be touched by the conceptions of earlier Americans too. After a long walk under budding trees, he wrote:

Emerging from these woods toward the city, one sees the white dome of the capitol soaring over the green swell of earth immediately in front, and lifting its four thousand tons of iron gracefully and lightly into the air. Of all the sights in Washington, that which will survive longest in my memory is the vision of the great dome thus rising cloud-like above the hills.

For Burroughs, the wonders of a spring in Washington veiled whatever blemishes were inherent in the city's façade. Apparently they did not for other naturalists. Elliott Coues and D. Webster Prentiss could write in their *Avifauna Columbiana*, published in 1883 by the Smithsonian Institution, "Twenty or twenty-five years ago, with a population of about 60,000, the National Capital was a mud-puddle in winter, a dust-heap in summer, a cow-pen and pig-sty all the year round." Mark Twain agreed, having remarked in 1862 that if only the mud were slightly diluted the streets could serve as canals.

By 1883, however, Washington had grown into a city of 180,000 people and considerably altered itself. A new grid of streets and sewers was laid. The springs, often polluted, were mostly abandoned, and a fourteen-mile aqueduct was built to bring drinking water to the city from the area of Great Falls; at that point the river aerated and purified itself in its tumultuous rush to the coastal plain.

While Washington grew into its image as the federal city, the Potomac was changing too, but not always for the better. The river just below the White House had been a mile wide in 1792. Silt, eroded from the stripped hillsides and badly contoured farmlands in the interior, dropped out from the river's flow as it widened and slowed in the estuary below Great Falls, forming shallows and extensive marshes. Malarial mosquitoes bred in some of the marshes along Washington's shore before the offending wetlands were filled in. The Dyke Marsh, haunted by Louis Halle in the spring of 1945, had been formed even earlier, when eighteenth-century vessels sailing up the river to Georgetown and Alexandria jettisoned the rocks they had carried as ballast across the ocean. These rocks formed a dike, behind which the marsh slowly grew and flourished.

As late as 1830, oceangoing vessels were able to navigate the Anacostia River, just below Washington, all the way to the old tobacco port of Bladensburg at the head of tidewater, six miles above its confluence with the Potomac. The Anacostia began to silt up too. By the 1880s only scows and other flat-bottomed boats could manage its shallow water. Yet it was these man-made marshes that were in part responsible for the city's teeming birdlife, providing food and sport for Washingtonians during the nineteenth century and spectacles for adherents of less lusty pleasures in our own time.

Wild rice abounded in the once-extensive marshes around Washington. Here birds of all kinds came to feed, nest, and rest. Swallows gathered in the feathery grass during migration, long-billed marsh wrens mated in the cat-tails, rails built their nests in grasses that supported them over the water, and herons fed in the shallows on plump frogs and other aquatic prey. In winter, after the pondweeds, eelgrass, and other water plants had died and submerged, ducks came in their thousands to dabble and dip.

Late in the summer and fall the marshes began to fill with human life too. Narrow streams called "guts" interlaced the marshes, ebbing and flowing with the tide, and along these lily-padded avenues hunters poled their boats in search of the flocks of migrating birds. Many of the gunners shot game for the markets. Thrushes (including robins), meadowlarks, woodpeckers, and even hawks and owls could be seen hanging for sale in the stalls during the fall migration. Tastiest of all to the local palates were bobolinks, called "reed-birds" in the fall after the males had lost their distinctive white-above, black-below breeding plumage and became indistinguishable from the brown-striped females. Coues and Prentiss, in their *Avifauna Columbiana*, singled them out on this account:

> The familiar "clink" of the Reed-bird begins to be heard over the tracts of wild oats along the river banks about the 20th of August, and from that time until October the restaurants are all supplied with Reed-birds—luscious morsels when genuine, but a great many Blackbirds and English sparrows are devoured by accomplished gourmands, who nevertheless do not know the difference when the bill of fare is printed correctly and the charges are sufficiently exorbitant.

They went on to describe the scene on the Anacostia marshes near Bennings Bridge, which crossed the river about two miles above the Navy Yard:

During the fall migrations these marshes afford refuge and food for innumerable hosts of Rails, Reed-birds and Red-winged Blackbirds, which attract scores of gunners, so that during the early days of September this locality reminds one of the firing of a skirmish line preceding a great battle. The crack of fowling-pieces is incessant from early morning to twilight. All classes in society are represented, from the gentleman sportsman with his pusher and favorite breech-loader, hunting Rail, to the ragged contraband with the cheap, old-fashioned, single-barreled muzzle-loader, or old style army musket, "wading" the marshes from knee to waist deep, to whom all flesh is game, who takes in principally Blackbirds and Reed-birds, and is particularly happy when he can surprise an unsophisticated Rail on the side of a "gut." The professional or market-gunner is also well represented, and during the early days of the season reaps a good harvest. It is a common thing on the first day of the season for one gunner to secure from twelve to twenty dozen Carolina Rail [soras, or "ortolans"] and as many Reed-birds. These birds are protected by law until September 1.

It is a rather comical sight to witness the gathering of the clans at Bennings' Bridge on the 1st day of September, preparatory to the slaughter of the innocents. As the light begins to appear in the east a motley line of sportsmen may be seen sitting upon the rail of the bridge waiting for sufficient light to see to shoot, dressed in all manner of costumes, and armed with all sorts of blunderbusses; some who have had the means and forethought to engage a skiff and pusher are off in style with the tide, others go in couples and skiffs and push each other, while the rabble, who constitute the great majority, take to the marshes and wade.

The narrow sixteen-foot skiffs, pointed at both ends and curved on the bottom to ease their passage over the marshy tangles, offered a precarious perch to the uninitiated sportsman. Both occupants had to stand, the sportsman to shoot over the high grasses, and the pusher to propel the boat with his long pole, crotched at the point to keep it from sinking into the gulping mud. Excellent balance was required of both men; as the pushers used to say, "You must part your hair in the middle." The pusher stopped when the sportsman found a target, then got out and retrieved the bird (or sometimes the sportsman).

Songbirds invaded the city's backyards and tree-lined streets, but in those days before modern optical instruments became generally available they were often difficult to see in the dense shrubbery or the treetops. The cardinal and the mockingbird, now probably the most prominent native American birds in the city, were considered comparatively rare before the end of the century. No wonder the cardinal was shy, for as John Burroughs reported, "It is much sought after by bird fanciers, and by boy gunners."

Those much-maligned aliens, the English (or house) sparrows, appeared in Washington about 1870 and soon became a conspicuous part of the city scene. Mrs. L. W. Maynard, a local ornithologist, expressed the common feeling about these birds, which had been imported from England to New York's Central Park and quickly increased their numbers and spread throughout most of the country. "English sparrows are generally regarded as an unmitigated nuisance," she wrote, "but in spite of their noise and filth, if they could be kept in check they might be tolerated in the city, where they give a certain life to the streets and parks and furnish some entertainment to children and house-bound invalids." But she was implacably set against their presence in the suburbs, where they drove away other nesting birds and ate buds and fruit; she recommended an occasional shotgun blast at them, and the pulling down of their nests.

Coues and Elliott betrayed no such tolerance. These irascible gentlemen wrote:

> Washington harbors and encourages a select assortment of noise-nuisances. The black newspaper imps who screech everyone deaf on Sunday morning; the fresh-fish fiends, the berry brutes, the soap-fat scoundrels, and the o' clo' devils; the milk mercenaries with their detonating gongs, but all these have their exits as well as their entrances; the Sparrows alone are tireless, ubiquitous, sempiternal. . . . In place of many sweet songsters which used to grace and enliven our streets, we have these animated manure machines, as almost every houseowner in the city knows to his cost.

Bird lovers had their innings for almost ten days during the early part of May in 1882. A cold rain in the Appalachians and to the north of Washington bottled up the northward migration, funneling a "tidal wave" of songbirds into the city in search of food. Scarlet tanagers, indigo buntings, thrushes, and warblers of all kinds were seen everywhere. Orioles walked over the grass like starlings. The birds were so numerous and so apparent even to the most inattentive city dwellers that a rumor circulated that a cargo of tropical birds had escaped from a ship tied up at a Georgetown wharf. One little boy shot six rose-breasted grosbeaks.

Probably no one of his time felt Washington's wildness more keenly, or took more advantage of it, than Theodore Roosevelt during his two administrations (1901–9). Historians often overlook the side of Roosevelt that dwelt on small things. The image of the Rough Rider, the "butcher of big game," the swashbuckler with the Big Stick, all engulf the man who could name the wildflowers of the fields and who, at least according to his sister Corinne, once broke into a cabinet meeting with the breathless announcement, "Gentlemen, do you know what happened this morning? I just saw a chestnut-sided warbler—and this is only February!"

It must be said that in his official residence he had a marvelous opportunity to see birds of all kinds from his window. Yet few Presidents before or since have made quite that kind of use of the White House grounds, with their lush plantings of redbuds, maples, and a variety of shrubs attractive to songbirds.

Roosevelt kept a list of the birds he observed, which he turned over to Mrs. Maynard for her book on the *Birds of Washington and Vicinity*, with such notes as: "Sparrow Hawk. A pair spent the last two winters on and around the White House grounds, feeding on the sparrows—largely, thank Heaven, on the English sparrows." The list came to fifty-six different species on the grounds, and he added, "Doubtless this list is incomplete; I have seen others that I have forgotten." Indeed he had; he forgot to tabulate all those English sparrows that were eaten by sparrow hawks. Roosevelt might be gratified now that local bird watchers have begun to make an annual Christmas Bird Count at the White House. The sparrow hawk was still about in 1973, but so were the English sparrows, seventy-nine of them in all, which made them the most numerous species.

The vigorous President often took a few hours away from his duties to hike along Rock Creek or through the bottomlands of the Potomac. On those hikes he indulged his passion for exercise while carrying out his determined plan to sort out all the colorful wood warblers, "exquisite little birds," he wrote, "but not conspicuous as a rule, except perhaps the blackburnian, whose brilliant orange throat and breast flame when they catch the sunlight as he flits among the trees."

Sometimes he was defeated by his own exuberance. He invited his old friend John Burroughs on a bird walk along Rock Creek. "We saw no birds," Burroughs reported afterward. "They could not keep up with us." Another frequent companion on his hikes was Gifford Pinchot, chief of the United States Forest Service and a prominent conservationist (in fact, Pinchot brought the word conservation, with its present meaning, into general use). Because they were likely to shake off the Secret Service men assigned to guard the President, Roosevelt and Pinchot each carried a pistol.

On one such strenuous hike along the Potomac, Roosevelt led his party through a swamp and then waist deep into the river itself. The bedraggled

but aristocratic Pinchot finally returned late in the afternoon to the elegant
house on Rhode Island Avenue where he lived with his mother.

"As I ran up the stairs to my room," Pinchot recalled, "my old nurse, Mary McCadden, who had been with me since I was eleven weeks old, was standing with her hand on the newel post. I rubbed my wet sleeve across it. She turned like a flash, pointed her finger at me in reproof, and exclaimed, 'You've been out with that President!'"

Roosevelt was just one of a growing number of men and women in the Washington area who were taking an interest in birds as sprightly, beautiful creatures rather than simply as objects for sport or the pot. In 1897 one of the first Audubon Societies in the country was created in the District of Columbia. George Miller Sternberg, the Surgeon General of the United States Army, was elected its president, and Roosevelt, while an Assistant Secretary of the Navy, soon became one of its honorary vice-presidents. The impetus for the organization of this Audubon Society, as for all others, was the appalling slaughter of herons, egrets, gulls, terns, and other birds by millinery gunners who wanted to have their plumage to stick about as decorations on women's hats. When Frank M. Chapman, the noted ornithologist, came down from New York's American Museum of Natural History to give the society's first public lecture, he chose the theme, "Woman As a Bird Enemy."

Both birds and the Audubon Society throve in Washington's green acres. Songbirds sought food, cover, and nesting places among the abundant trees and shrubs. In 1928 a hurricane carried torrential rains into the city, filling the excavation for a new building which was to house the Department of Commerce, then presided over by Herbert Hoover. Residents and government workers were treated to an extraordinary invasion of plovers, ruddy turnstones, sanderlings, and other shorebirds attracted to the instant aquatic habitat provided by "Hoover's Lake."

During World War II, when most such organizations languished, Washington's Audubon Society went through a renaissance. Many of the nation's leading ornithologists came to Washington on various wartime jobs and managed to fit in such bird-watching expeditions as were posible during those days of strict gasoline rationing. Rachel Carson, Roger Tory Peterson, Joseph J. Hickey, Shirley A. Briggs, John W. Aldrich, and, of course, Louis Halle, drawn together by the tide of events, helped to build a strong Audubon Naturalist Society under the presidency of Irston R. Barnes.

Even after World War II, hawks hunted openly for pigeons and small birds in downtown Washington. According to Barnes, two peregrine falcons staked out their territory between Pennsylvania and Constitution avenues in 1946, a Cooper's hawk hunted at Fifteenth Street and Pennsylvania Avenue, and sharp-shinned hawks patrolled LaFayette Square. Fish crows controlled pigeons downtown by raiding their nests on the ledges of hotels and government buildings.

The large urban population of English sparrows had been sustained chiefly by the horse-and-buggy civilization. There was plenty of sparrow food to be found in the copious horse droppings on downtown streets and around stables where horses were fed. As horses disappeared from the city with the advent of the motorcar the sparrows themselves diminished. Gone were those roosting sites which a government publication had described as "avian ghettos crammed with greedy, filthy, bickering clouds of a single alien species." But in 1912 another alien species, the starling, likewise imported to this country from England by some foolish bird enthusiasts during the last century, arrived in Washington, and four years later they were breeding there. Today they are a prominent Washington spectacle, like cherry trees and Congressmen. By day they fan out over the countryside in search of food, then return to the city in the evening to roost in creaking thousands on the convenient ledges and cornices of government buildings. During the cold months they are able to extract warmth from these buildings, and government workers have been waging incessant war on them for years.

Other birds have not been able to adapt to encroaching civilization. There has long been a tendency by man to fill in the marshes around Washington for development, or even for dumps. As late as 1968 the House Interior Committee received a favorable staff report on a move to turn the Featherstone Marsh across from Mason Neck into a sanitary landfill, the staff's ecological illiterates reporting that the area was "marshy, and hence unusable in its present condition."

Louis Halle's old haunt, Dyke Marsh, has been acquired by the National Park Service, although intermittent dredging for sand and gravel has taken place there because of an agreement with the former owners. The badly polluted Anacostia River has lost much of its marshland too, though here and there among its obsolescent industrial sites the river's floodplains have been renewed as parkland. Washington, in fact, has never forgotten it had a river. Most American cities which owed their very existence to a river promptly defaced and polluted its shores so badly that they were forced to turn their backs on it, leaving the riverfront to industries and railroad tracks. Washington opened itself more to the Potomac's amenities. In some places its planners provided parks and parkways with broad views of the river. It has not always been their fault that the tyrannical automobile proliferated in numbers that defile the river in their own way.

On the whole, though, developers, highway builders, and purblind city planners did their best to stamp out the Washington that L'Enfant envisioned and that John Burroughs, Theodore Roosevelt, Louis Halle, and thousands of others treasured. Sometimes Washington looks like all the other great cities we have blighted. Even the thirty or more unique magnolia bogs, so called because of the swamp or sweetbay magnolia (*Magnolia virginiana*) which was their dominant shrub, are almost wholly submerged in the city's environs under paving and buildings.

But the greenery and the birds still have a foot solidly wedged in the door. They remain a subversive force that needs only small encouragement to recapture for Washington that bright aura which Louis Halle mirrored in his book.

The Potomac reflects the night lights of the nation's capital. Under cover of darkness, the night creatures leave their daytime hiding places: barn owls from the Smithsonian Institution patrol the mall; bats from the lofts of historic buildings hawk insects over the Lincoln Memorial, while nighthawks scoop up moths at the Washington Monument; and the night serenade of the mockingbird sounds through the Capitol grounds.

Daisy fleabane blooms in waste fields and along roadsides throughout the area. Its dainty blossoms first appear in June and last until early autumn. It is a favorite plant of the eastern tailed blue butterfly. Fleabanes, at least in name, have the reputation of being natural insect repellants.

Nature wastes nothing. In the death of one species she gives life to another, and in that one's death others take life. Nowhere is this more evident than on the floor of the forest, as in moss growing on a decaying log in Rock Creek Park.

In that last splendid moment before winter, a tree reaches the peak of loveliness. It is the grandest link of a miraculous chain. The blossoms have fed the insects that pollinated them; the leaves have unfurled to make food for the growing fruits; in their ripeness the fruits have fed the wood thrush; the seeds have been sown and the tree has laid down another ring; and now the leaves die in a final burst of color. These tupelo and maple trees line Washington's Indian Head Highway.

Most of the freshwater marshes along the Anacostia are gone today, with their pond-weeds and grasses and "Carolina rails" and "reed-birds," but a few spots remain to remind us of the Anacostia as it was in the time of Elliot Coues and Webster Prentiss.

Snowy egrets and other species were nearly wiped out by market hunters near the end of the last century. The gracefully shaped and delicately textured plumes, known as aigrettes, were sold to milliners for use as decorations on women's hats. As a result, several bird protective groups were formed which finally succeeded in eliminating the vicious trade. One of the oldest of these is Washington's Audubon Naturalist Society. Today the society is a strong force in conservation along the Potomac.

The peregrine falcon is a hawk of rocky cliffs and promontories from which it rushes forth to capture smaller birds. In a stoop (dive) on prey, this bird can reach speeds of 200 miles per hour. In 1946, two peregrines staked out a territory on the rocklike promontories of Washington's federal buildings. Today the peregrine is extinct as a breeding bird in the eastern United States, largely because of persistent pesticides.

Spring beauties are among the earliest of spring flowers, not only in Washington but throughout the Potomac watershed. In some places they are so abundant that they form a white carpet on the forest floor. The root is a cherry-sized edible tuber, tasting much like a potato.

The river displays its awesome power as it carves away the rocks at Great Falls. In a final burst of white water, it descends from the rocky piedmont to the slow-moving tidewater pools of the coastal plain. Though the fall line which separates the piedmont and coastal plain passes through the city of Washington, the erosive power of the river has moved the falls thirteen miles upstream.

Tiniest of all shorebirds is the least sandpiper. A bare five inches in length, it is found on mudflats and in wet meadows and potholes along the Potomac during spring and fall migration. It is often seen in the Washington area at turf farms, Dyke Marsh, and Bolling Field.

An ancient beech is a tree to treasure, a tree of the "wild" places in and around the city. Each wound or lost limb scar has its own characteristic pattern of furrows and ridges, showing the great life force within the tree. Beeches have become America's favorite carving trees, covered with Cupid's hearts, initials, and dates. In spite of this, they survive. In winter, they hold their leaves until the fresh spring growth loosens their grip. The silver-gray bark is the finest shade of gray in all of nature.

Rock Creek Park is a continuing source of delight for nature-loving Washingtonians. John Burroughs, Theodore Roosevelt, Gifford Pinchot, and Louis Halle came here to escape the tensions of Washington bureaucracy; although traversed by a heavily used highway today, the park retains much of its wildness. For modern visitors there are still bits of woodsy beauty such as this fungus on a fallen river birch, Polystictus versicolor.

The black-crowned night heron is a creature of freshwater marshes and shallow backwaters. It is most often seen flying to and from the feeding grounds at dusk and dawn. Around the city it is seen at Roaches Run, and Louis Halle reported a daytime roost in Rock Creek Park.

PART III

THE CANAL

The lust to expand is a characteristic note sounded in American history. From the earliest colonial times ships sailed up the Potomac's estuary as far as they were able, that ultimate point eventually being marked by the new ports of Alexandria and Georgetown, staring jealously at each other from opposite shores. Beyond, the ships encountered the river in tumult as it dropped at the fall line from the hard rocks of the piedmont plateau to the soft and eroded base of the coastal plain. Great Falls seemed to be an enduring barrier to heavy transportation.

This is not to say that there was no traffic between the various regions of the Potomac Valley. Both the Indians and the early frontiersmen traveled back and forth along the Potomac and its tributaries (especially the Shenandoah and the Monocacy) in canoes, and there was a network of comparatively busy trails throughout most of the East. The Indian routes generally cut straight through the wilderness, not meandering from town to town around farms and natural features as those of the white man did later on; though often extensive windfalls (like that for which the Battle of Fallen Timbers was named) provided sudden obstacles. Yet even for men on horseback there was a limit to the amount of goods they could transport up and down the valley.

The colonists' lust to expand intensified during the eighteenth century. Increasingly, planters and traders looked to the West for wealth, or at least for a good living, as they faced the portents of financial ruin on the tobacco plantations. In 1748 the tidewater planters organized the Ohio Company to exploit the plentiful land and furs that were available in the mountains and beyond. The company's aggressive policies (supported by the Crown) antagonized the French and fueled the quarrel that led to the French and Indian Wars.

The Ohio Company's own light went out during the Revolution, but it had kindled a more lasting one. Among the planter families which owned shares in the company were the Washingtons, old Augustine and his sons, Lawrence and George. Like the others, they were aware of the obstacles that interrupted the free exchange of goods between East and West. There were Frenchmen and Indians, of course, but they would be swept aside in time. *61*

More adamant were the rocks at Great Falls, the residue of ancient mountains. How were boats to surmount that 3,600-foot interval in the navigable flow that abruptly lowered the river by nearly eighty feet?

In 1754, when he was only twenty-two years old, George Washington began to consider the possibility of skirting the falls with a canal. The young man already knew the Potomac Valley well, having served as a surveyor for the Ohio Company. He and a few friends were convinced that only such an audacious undertaking as the construction of a canal would fulfill the valley's destiny as a conduit between the colonies and the riches to the west. No one in America had ever built a canal, nor had the great age of canals begun even in the British Isles.

A Potomac canal remained a dream until after the Revolution, when Washington revived the idea. In 1784 the tidewater gentry organized the Potowmack Company for the purpose of building a series of short canals. Thomas Jefferson proposed Washington as the company's first president, and from then until the end of his life Washington took a keen interest in the progress of this monumental undertaking, seeing the canal not only as a great commercial and engineering venture but, more important, as a means of creating unity within the young country.

Work began in 1785, mostly by slaves and indentured laborers. Washington himself spent much time at Great Falls before he became the President of the new nation, putting up with many hardships to be on the scene even during the dirtiest winter weather. In his diary he described a February inspection of the falls "after as disagreeable ride as I ever had for the distance." Gangs of workers removed rocks and sand from the river's channel and built dams to raise by a few inches the level of the water. They dug five sections of canal along the northern shore, six feet deep and twenty or twenty-five feet wide, the banks sometimes raised by earth or rocks, to circumvent particularly rugged stretches of the river at various points from Little Falls to beyond Harpers Ferry. Perhaps the most impressive part of this early American engineering feat was the series of locks that raised or lowered the boats along the canal. Walled with huge hand-hewn blocks of sandstone, the locks were twelve or fourteen feet wide and about one hundred feet long.

Washington did not live to see the canal finished. It came to a completion of sorts in 1802, permitting "gondolas" and other primitive craft to make the trip from western Maryland to Georgetown with furs, grain, lumber, flour, and, sometimes, mountain whiskey. The boats were about seventy-five feet long and could carry one hundred tons of goods. Many of them were too frail to absorb the pounding they would take as they were poled back upstream against the rushing river, and so they were broken up at Georgetown and sold for lumber. But for much of the year even the sturdier flat-bottomed boats lay idle. They were not able to negotiate the shallow places in the river once the spring freshets had diminished; thus cargoes were not delivered on schedule and the Potowmack Company lost the anticipated tolls that would have made the venture profitable. The Maryland and Virginia legislatures revoked the company's charter in 1821.

It was not in the spirit of the confident young nation to admit defeat even at the hands of a mighty river. A way to link East and West would be found, and obviously it lay along the same path taken by Washington's primitive and inadequate canal. The Industrial Revolution was under way, and engineers on both sides of the Atlantic were beginning to flex their muscles. Leading proponents of canals in England included Josiah Wedgwood, the potter, and Erasmus Darwin, the poet and inventor who was the grandfather of the immortal Charles and who envisioned canals "parting the velvet meads" throughout his country. In the United States, work on the Erie Canal had already begun. This immense project eventually stretched 363 miles from Albany to Buffalo and beyond, providing a direct route to the West and playing a vital role in making New York the greatest American port. The Erie Canal opened in 1825.

As the Erie neared completion there was anxiety in cities such as Baltimore and Georgetown that they would be entirely superseded as major ports and trading centers by New York. Their businessmen decided to take over the rights of the old Potowmack Company and build a new canal over its route. They organized the Chesapeake and Ohio Canal Company in 1828, and on July 4 of that year President John Quincy Adams turned the first spadeful of earth (after twice hitting a stump) at Little Falls and the project was under way. Adams compared it in advance to the building of the pyramids and the Colossus of Rhodes.

The canal's promoters intended to push it eventually all the way to the Ohio River at Pittsburgh. But the obstacles in its path, many of them not considered at the time, were formidable and, in the end, nearly fatal. Money was not a problem at first, but labor was. The new company sent agents to the British Isles to engage laborers to work under terms of indenture. Many of these men had already worked as navvies (a humorous reference to them as "navigators"), excavating canals in England. More than a thousand English and Irish laborers agreed to come for legally specified periods. The agents also sent back skilled English and Welsh stonecutters, many of whom were to leave their trademarks in the great stones of which the locks and lockhouses were built along the Potomac. And so, more than a century before the United

States triggered a "brain drain," English engineers could very well have complained of a "muscle drain."

The building of the canal and its brief golden age provide a colorful strand in the fabric of American history. At times the gangs of Irish workmen seemed to be more of a liability than an asset. The lack of enthusiasm for the job proved infectious and they defected in large numbers, often to be brought back by force to complete the terms of their contract. Fierce battles broke out between rival gangs. In 1834 the men of County Cork did battle with County Longford men; five were killed and dozens of others injured. Another bloodletting took place a year or two later, when shanties were burned and canal property destroyed. Like rival armies the combatants appointed guards and night patrols to protect their encampments.

At one point the Canal Company tried to impose "prohibition" on the workers, but it was as unsuccessful as the great experiment closer to our own time. Drunkenness only increased. Deprived of their liquor during the day, many of the workers spent all night at the nearest tavern, drinking and breaking heads. Prohibition was abruptly rescinded. Even more disruptive than alcohol were the terrible epidemics of cholera that erupted in the filthy shanty towns. The good people of Hagerstown, Maryland, finally protested to the company because of the number of Irish funerals held there, fearing both contagion from the diseased and mayhem from the riotous mourners, and Catholic cemeteries were provided closer to the canal.

Somehow the work went forward, and by 1831 a section of the canal was opened between Georgetown and Seneca Falls. But trouble mounted. The company was using up its capital much faster than it had anticipated, so the state of Maryland intervened occasionally to rescue the company with further infusions of cash. A constant worry was a parallel line on the map— the Baltimore & Ohio Railroad, racing the canal toward the mountains. The two projects had started construction simultaneously in 1828 and chose the same path up the Maryland side of the river. (This rivalry in construction was to be equaled by the competition for cargoes, once both were completed; the railroad was to win the race to the mountains by eight years and, much later, to win the ultimate battle for survival.) The space between them blurred at the narrow part of the Potomac Valley between Point of Rocks and Harpers Ferry, and a heated controversy over rights-of-way ensued. The opening of the canal to that point was delayed until 1833, when the two companies settled the legal issues.

In 1839 the canal, hugging the river's shore, extended some 135 miles from Georgetown to the area west of Hancock, Maryland, but there it bogged down in financial woes. It took eleven years to push on the final 50 miles to Cumberland in the Alleghenies. This city, founded by the Ohio Company in 1749, became the center of the transmontane trade. It was notable as a transfer point, particularly of coal, to the boats which would take the cargoes down the canal.

The people of Cumberland bitterly resisted every attempt to push the canal (fed by other rivers) toward the Ohio, rightly fearing that their city's *raison d'être* would disappear. Still, the calls for an extension of the canal continued with diminishing fervor into the 1870s. Whatever enthusiasm there was for the costly process of carving a canal through the mountains seems to have been generated by the knowledge that the tunnels would have to be bored through rich coal seams; the bargemen, so the story went, would simply gather up the coal as they proceeded through the tunnels and the project would pay for itself! But the extension plans were dropped, and the canal's course was complete.

By this time the Irish voices raised in revelry and the horrors of the shanty towns were only disquieting memories. Canal days, as they come down to us in stories and pictures, retain an aura of tranquillity. Occasionally a train would rumble past, its tracks separated from the canal embankments for part of the way only by a strip of gravel. For the rest, it was an atmosphere for the painters of idylls.

There was the peaceful flow of water through the canal itself, a counterpoint to the river, marbled with foam, which rushed along beside it. The canal ranged in width from fifty to eighty feet and was from six to eight feet deep, but the seventy-five locks determined the width of the boats that navigated its 189 miles. These stone enclosures were one hundred feet long and fifteen feet wide, with swinging wooden gates (of a type invented by Leonardo da Vinci) at both ends to regulate the level of the water inside. The barges, then, were usually ninety feet or a little more in length, while their beam was restricted to fourteen and a half feet. They carried up to 130 tons of goods on the trip from Cumberland, which might take a week or ten days to complete.

The barges ran on mule power. Two or three mules, plodding along the towpath beside the canal and often led by one of the barge captain's children, pulled craft, crew, passengers, and cargo. Sometimes they also pulled the off-duty mules, which occupied a forward enclosure. A laden barge traveling downstream had the right of way over one coming up the canal, which dropped its towlines into the water to avoid entanglements as they passed. A blast from the captain's horn alerted the lockkeeper to a barge's approach. In winter the canal was closed to protect the locks from ice.

Packet boats, providing meals and cabins for their fifty or sixty passengers, regularly plied the canal between Georgetown and Cumberland. Apparently this means of travel was not always a delight. Mrs. Frances Trollope, during her years in America, had some experience with canal packet boats. After a trip on the Erie Canal on which she was squeezed and jostled in the all-purpose cabin with people who seemed to her to act "upon a system of unshrinking egotism," she wrote, "With a very delightful party of one's own choosing, fine temperate weather, and a strong breeze to chase the mosquitoes, this mode of traveling might be very agreeable, but I can hardly imagine any motive of convenience powerful enough to induce me again to imprison myself in a canal boat under ordinary circumstances."

Charles Dickens apparently went through similar discomforts, but he accepted them more agreeably. In his *American Notes* he wrote, "There was much in this mode of traveling which I heartily enjoyed at the time, and look back upon with great pleasure."

The canal's troubles, however, did not end with its completion to Cumberland. Nature was to deliver the final blow. Periodic floods left long segments of the canal in ruins. In 1875 barges carried one million tons of coal from the mountains. But in 1889 a great flood all but obliterated the canal. The Baltimore & Ohio Railroad bought out its stricken competitor at this point, chiefly to preserve the right-of-way, and invested in its restoration. But the canal was not able to survive the competition of the railroads themselves. It limped along, losing money and gradually decaying toward a picturesque ruin until 1924, when another catastrophic flood put an end to it; fourteen years later, the old ditch was taken over and partly restored by the federal government.

In its ruin the canal contributes as great a service to the people of the Potomac as it did during those years when mules pulled the West's wealth to Georgetown. As the area in and around Washington succumbs to concrete and fumes, the canal and its towpath remain a ribbon of life reaching toward the mountains. Many wild plants have been preserved along the canal from grazing, agriculture, and building, just as they were preserved along railroad tracks on western prairies and in the crumbling walls of old churches and castles in Europe. The towpath has survived as a broad trail along the canal, wide enough so that hikers may walk abreast and firm enough on its gravel base and chipped-stone surface to permit bicycle traffic. Winding through the Potomac's bottomlands, the towpath leads hikers into rich deciduous woods of sycamore, beech, elm, tulip, and river birch and past an often dense understory of box elder, spicebush, and, unfortunately, poison ivy. This is one of the fabled "birding" areas in the East. Prothonotary warblers sing their vigorous little songs from the thickets along the canal. Blue-gray gnatcatchers rasp and wheeze overhead. The parula warbler, which in the South builds

its intricate pocketlike nests of Spanish moss and in the North of the stringy
gray tree lichen called old-man's beard, here sometimes nests in the flood debris that clings to the lower branches of shrubs after the water subsides.

In the early 1950s the state planners, in a fit of dottiness exceptional even for them, conceived a plan to unroll a new highway along the route conveniently provided by the towpath and canal. After all, it was nothing but useless space, they reasoned. Even the Washington newspapers took up the call in the name of progress. Supreme Court Justice William O. Douglas read the editorials with understandable outrage and immediately issued a challenge to the offending editors. Why not walk with me the length of the canal, Douglas asked, and see for yourselves the beauty we stand to lose? As in a sentimental movie, the Justice's appeal touched hearts that had been hardened by practicality, and the editors took up the challenge. They would follow Douglas on foot all the way from Cumberland to Washington, 189 miles. To publicize Douglas's call to save the canal, other interested people agreed to hike too.

In March 1954 a motley collection of editors, conservationists, photographers, and even a couple of dogs set out on the memorable walk. It lasted eight days. A few of the less hardy dropped out along the way, but as the hikers approached Washington they were joined by latecomers, eager to be in at the finish. The National Park Service provided a sightseeing barge, towed by a pair of mules, for the footsore. As Douglas entered the city, still on foot, his band became, in the words of one awed observer, "a triumphal procession, suggestive of Cleopatra's retinue on the Nile."

Douglas had made his point. The press reversed its stand, a public clamor arose, and the highway builders slunk away. The federal government designated the old canal a national monument and, finally, a national historic park. Each year, on the anniversary of Douglas's march, hundreds of other hikers take to the towpath in a lighthearted reenactment of what had been a deadly serious business.

And the prothonotary warblers still sing from their perches in thickets along the towpath of the C. and O. Canal.

Lock No. 20 at Great Falls is one of the few on the Chesapeake and Ohio Canal which have been restored. The locks were used to raise or lower the canal barges. For barges going upstream, the downstream gate was opened while the upstream gate was closed. The barge moved into the lock and the lower gate was closed. Then the upstream gate was opened to fill the lock with water. The rising water floated the barge to the upstream level, where it resumed its trip. For downstream barges, the process was reversed.

Skunk cabbage, for those who haunt the woods year round, belies its derogatory name. Its flower livens the dull winter months along the canal with a promise of spring, and the brilliant green of its giant summer leaf dresses the wet woodlands where it grows. Blooming in winter, it has the distinction of being both the first and the last flower of the year.

An aqueduct crosses Fifteen Mile Creek near Little Orleans, Maryland. Just as highway bridges are used to carry a road across a stream, aqueducts were used to carry the canal over the Potomac's tributaries. In an age of concrete, the graceful arches of weathered native stone bring welcome relief to the eye.

With a delicate hand nature casts a snowflake, paints the frosted window, and sculpts the frozen stream. Her works are on exhibit everywhere, at all times, and the exhibit is constantly changed. Ice formations such as these can be seen on the many small streams along the canal.

Before the leafing of the trees, when the earth soaks up the warmth of the spring sun, the orange-red fluids of the bloodroot flow. In April, along with white and blue hepaticas and yellow trout lilies, bloodroot blooms in the wild gardens that cover the rocky slopes above the canal.

In winter, evening grosbeaks sometimes invade the
Potomac Valley in large numbers. From Maine, New
Brunswick, Nova Scotia, and other northern breeding
places, they come as the winter food crop disappears.
They are birds of the open woodlands and forest edges.
Birders along the canal often hear their sparrowlike
chatter as they fly overhead or see them on feeders of
homes near the canal. They will visit a feeder all winter
long if provided with sunflower seeds.

In the early days of March when gloves and warm boots
are still comfortable, the first sweet song of the field sparrow
is heard in the open areas along the canal. Most often the
bird is seen in abandoned fields overgrown with broom
sedges and dotted by small red cedars. It is this stage of
succession in the return from plowed field to climax forest
that the field sparrow finds necessary for its well-being. Its
nest is sometimes on the ground but is most often in a low
shrub or tree, as here in a multiflora rose.

The crimson-eyed rose mallow is a showy flower of the marsh-lands and wet places in late summer. In winter the seed heads lend a graceful elegance to the canal near Seneca, Maryland.

Many of the locks are reverting to nature. The
wooden parts are largely gone. Algae, lichens,
and mosses grow on the cut stonework, and
ferns have gained a foothold in the joints.
How marvelous this process! Just as the
ancient mountains were prepared for the
climax forest by these primitive plants, so now
nature begins the long process of reclaiming
the stone handiwork of the mason. The lichens
exude their acids to make soil from the rock.
The mosses take hold and add their humus,
and on it goes until . . . the forest.

The mason who uses native stone practices
genuine art. Weathered by wind and water,
touched by lichens and mosses, these stones
are the best works of man and nature. The
orderly geometry and rich earthy colors blend
in harmony with the scene. They belong here
like the Deptford pinks and the oxeye daisies
by the towpath.

Across from the town of Paw Paw, West Virginia, the mountain meets the river. It was easier to go under than over, so a tunnel was blasted through the rock large enough for both the canal and the towpath. Today hikers and bikers still follow the towpath through the tunnel.

*The first rains of Hurricane Agnes have just fallen. Now in the translucent
magic of fresh water the colors of nature come into their own. Living greens,
yellows, and rich grays and browns catch the light where a few minutes
before a colorless rock had lain. This fallen piece of the mountain lies at the
entrance to Paw Paw tunnel.*

*A stone stairway climbs the side of the canal to the top of Paw Paw tunnel.
As if by plan, a display of Christmas fern has wedged itself in the cracks at
the mountainside. Christmas fern is green all winter long and was used for
yuletide decorations. Remembering that the leaflets are shaped like a
Christmas stocking makes this the easiest of all ferns to identify.*

Downstream, leaving Paw Paw tunnel, the sides of the canal were steep and of solid rock with no place for a towpath, so a wooden pathway was built above the canal. This section has been restored.

PART IV

THE LAND
ABOVE THE FALLS

In the eighteenth century, failing planters, landless tidewater families, and adventurous hunters began to filter through the gaps in the higher country in western Virginia and Maryland. Many of these people migrated up the Potomac and began a new page of American history, mingling among the ridges and valleys with Scotch-Irish and German immigrants coming through broad valleys from Pennsylvania. They left behind them the pines and exhausted lands of the coastal plain to live among the hardwood forests and rich limestone soils of the interior. And though they also left behind them the glamour of plantation society, they created an independent and vigorous civilization of their own, which was to flower in glory and then almost disintegrate in tragedy during the nineteenth century.

The land was good to the these newcomers in the regions beyond the Great Falls. The first of the geologic "provinces" they encountered was the piedmont plateau, rising above the coastal plain on its base of hard crystalline rocks, with good rolling farmland and lush forests. Many of the Potomac's chief tributaries enter it here, and their names ring with history: Bull Run, Antietam Creek, and the Monocacy, where Jubal Early's II Corps defeated a much larger Union force in 1864.

The Potomac is a great river even here, swollen by its tributaries and acquiring the gradient of a river after leaving its precipitous stream beds in the mountains to the west. Islands stud the river. The plants and animals differ from those that can withstand the fluctuations in salinity and temperature in the estuary; freshwater mussels find here the right combination of temperature, oxygen, bottom composition, and speed of water.

Beyond, and divided from the piedmont by the Blue Ridge, is the Great Valley of eastern North America, which extends from Alabama to Quebec. To the north this valley is called the Cumberland, and to the south it is the Tennessee. But at this point, where it stretches for thirty miles from North Mountain on the west to the Blue Ridge on the east, it is named for the lovely river that winds through its fertile limestone farmland—the Shenandoah.

The Shenandoah is the Potomac's largest tributary. The two historic rivers meet at Harpers Ferry, a historic name in its own right. No one has

described their confluence more feelingly than Thomas Jefferson did in
Notes on the State of Virginia:

> The passage of the Potomac through the Blue Ridge is, perhaps, one
> of the most stupendous scenes in nature. You stand on a very high point
> of land. On your right comes up the Shenandoah, having ranged along
> the foot of the mountains an hundred miles to seek a vent. On your left
> approaches the Potomac, in quest of a passage also. In the moment of
> their junction they rush together against the mountain, rend it asunder,
> and pass off to the sea.

Farms sprang up quickly in the piedmont and the hospitable valleys beyond it. The Indians were almost entirely pushed out of the Potomac region,
cattle were pastured in the natural meadows, and grains were planted in the
limestone soils. Here the newcomers sowed America's first major granary.
Wheat was the principal crop, though corn was also grown extensively. The
farmers battled insect pests and diseases, as well as a nearly catastrophic
erosion of the land brought on by their persistence in farming the steep
slopes in addition to the valley floors. But if their own ignorance sometimes
threatened to do them in, their courage and imagination created a new agricultural empire just as that of their forebears in the tidewater country had
created a new nation. They experimented with better seeds, they bred
sturdier cattle, they practiced contour cultivation to diminish the wear and
tear on the slopes.

Soil conservation took a great step forward in Virginia in 1803 with the
publication of John Binns's *Treatise of Practical Farming*, a pamphlet which
sold for fifty cents and in which Binns set forth the principles of the
"Loudoun system." His method included the addition of lime to grain fields
and the planting of cattle pastures to clover. This gospel of soil conservation
appeared just in time to save the farmlands of the piedmont. The people of the
upper Potomac were not going to destroy their soils as their fathers had in the
tidewater country.

But the genius of that country was far from exhausted. Within a few
years after Binns died in 1813 a man who was to become much more widely
known was already at work in his shop in the Shenandoah Valley, a few miles
to the west of Loudoun County. Robert McCormick, a blacksmith, and his
son, Cyrus, had already invented a variety of farm implements, including
a new type of plow and a threshing machine. But no one had been able to
solve the problem of reaping the wheat fields, growing more extensive each
year yet vulnerable upon ripening to sudden changes in the weather. Cyrus
kept on tinkering and in 1831 finally perfected the reaper which established

his abiding place in American history. The McCormick reaper cut as much wheat in a day as fifteen men were able to handle previously; added to the other horse-drawn machinery developed for use in the fields, it released the farmers of the upper Potomac from dependence on the hordes of slaves and indentured servants which had helped to ruin the tidewater planters. The upper Potomac Valley retained its supremacy as a granary until after the Civil War, when the great unbroken spaces of the West proved even more appropriate for the cultivation of wheat and corn.

Meanwhile, the various natural resources of the upper valley provided the basis for flourishing industries. Gristmills arose along many swift-flowing streams to grind corn and wheat. The forests of oak, walnut, and hickory that clothed the slopes were felled to supply wood for houses, boats, and a great many smaller items. In 1784 a merchant of Bremen, Germany, named John Frederick Amelung recruited a number of skilled glassmakers and sailed with them (in an entourage that included his large family and all their tutors and governesses) to augment his fortune in the New World. He bought land in the Potomac Valley at the mouth of Maryland's Monocacy River, acquired an interest in Washington's Potowmack Canal Company, named the site New Bremen, and set up a "glass manufactory." Potash for the manufacturing process was derived from the local forests. Praise for Amelung's glass bottles and goblets came from all who examined them. For ten years the New Bremen factory turned out the finest glass in America, but the competition from cheap English and Irish imports finally proved overwhelming. The glass factory closed, the artisans scattered to firms more securely financed, and, when a woolen mill took over the premises, New Bremen started life anew as Fleecy Dale.

Iron, appropriately, proved a hardier product in the Potomac Valley. Even before the Revolutionary War the ore that was readily available in the Maryland hills stimulated a thriving iron industry. Blast furnaces were built along Catoctin and Antietam creeks, processing the ore with the aid of lime from nearby outcrops and charcoal made from the region's copious supplies of wood. Waterpower ran the bellows and trip-hammers. The industry turned out a wide variety of products, from stoves to nails to parts for James Rumsey's pioneer steamboat (or "flying teakettle"), but none exerted so great an influence on the valley's subsequent history as gun barrels.

In 1796 the federal government purchased land at Harpers Ferry and established an armory there. The new armory imported pig iron by barge from the ironworks farther up the river. Its workmen assembled muskets and cannon and, later, the new breech-loading rifles. Harpers Ferry thus became the chief industrial town in the Potomac Valley. Situated on the imposing bluffs at the confluence of the Potomac and Shenandoah rivers, it could justly lay claim to being the valley's most picturesque town too.

It was on Harpers Ferry that John Brown turned his deranged attention in 1859. Whether Brown was a hero or a villain is still in dispute, but that he was mad there is no doubt. Born in Connecticut, he was a wanderer much of his life and consistently a failure in business enterprises. Abolition was the driving force of his life, and he became a part of the Underground Railroad that funneled fugitive slaves into Canada.

Like many fanatics, Brown possessed the gift of arousing fanatic devotion among his followers. Yet he was able to impress perfect strangers too. Richard Henry Dana, Jr., on a journey through the Adirondack Mountains in 1849, chanced upon the remote log cabin in which Brown was then living. Ten years later, when Brown's name sprang to the lips of almost every American, Dana was on the voyage that produced the background for his book *Two Years Before the Mast;* thus it was not until after the Civil War that he came to associate the John Brown whose body was already a-moldering in the grave with the intense, dignified man he had encountered in the Adirondacks. He went back to the journal he had kept in those days and found a reference to the early meeting:

> The place belonged to a man named Brown, originally from Berkshire in Massachusetts, a thin, sinewy, hard-favored, clear-headed, honest-minded man, who had spent all his days as a frontier farmer. On conversing with him, we found him well-informed on most subjects, especially in the natural sciences. He had books and evidently made a diligent use of them. Having acquired some property, he was able to keep a good farm and had confessedly the best cattle and the best farming utensils for miles round. His wife looked superior to the poor place they lived in, which was a cabin with only four rooms. She appeared to be out of health. He seemed to have an unlimited family of children, from a cheerful, nice, healthy woman of twenty or so, and a full-sized red-haired son who seemed to be the foreman of the farm, through every grade of boy and girl to a couple that could hardly speak plain.

But what apparently most impressed Dana was the fact that Brown had just brought a black couple with him to the farm; he had them to dinner at his table and also, in addressing them, prefixed a "Mr." and "Mrs." to their surnames.

"It was plain," Dana wrote, "that they had not been so treated or spoken to often before, perhaps never until that day, for they had all the awkwardness of field hands on a plantation; and what to do on the introduction was quite beyond their experiences."

Meanwhile, Brown had wandered from the Adirondacks and settled in Kansas during its bloody days. Here he found a more active mission than serving as a station on the Underground Railroad. When proslavery ruffians sacked the town of Lawrence in 1856, Brown came to see himself as an instrument in the hand of God. He led four of his sons and two other men on a reprisal raid, murdering five proslavery men on the banks of the Pottawatomie River; "to cause a restraining fear" were the words in which he justified the massacre.

Brown began to conceive a grandiose plan. He would lead an armed insurrection of the slaves, establishing a stronghold in the Southern mountains from which to carry on his holy war. In 1859 he rented a house near Harpers Ferry, whose arsenal as we have seen held a huge store of federal arms. On October 16 he moved to take over the town and the arsenal. The episode was brief and bloody. (Ironically, the first man killed was a black porter at the railroad station.) Brown achieved his objective, securing the town, but curiously settled down until his escape was cut off by the local militia. Government forces under Colonel Robert E. Lee attacked Brown's party at Harpers Ferry, killing ten of his men, and took the wounded Brown a prisoner. (John Wilkes Booth, later the perpetrator of the other great irrational act of the time, was a member of the Virginia militia company that captured Brown.) During his trial for treason Brown reverted to the "grave, serious man" whom Dana had met, defending his cause but not himself in fervent declamations. He was convicted and hanged.

The violence at Harpers Ferry led inexorably to the much greater violence of the Civil War, a story that reaches far beyond the area of our present concern. Yet no one can read that story without being aware that the Potomac River Valley was often the conflict's center stage. The river itself was the frontier between the contending forces. Many of the campaigns had as their objective the capture or the defense of the Baltimore & Ohio Railroad along its banks or the bridges that spanned its flow. The Potomac tributaries were the scenes of unforgettable battles. The name of General Philip H. Sheridan became as feared and hated in the Shenandoah Valley as that of Sherman in Georgia; sweeping through the Confederacy's "breadbasket" in 1864–65 at the head of the Army of the Shenandoah, Sheridan left such devastation of crops and livestock in his wake that he was able to say of the valley, "A crow couldn't fly through it without a haversack." The Potomac itself remained a focus of national attention right through the final tragedy, when John Wilkes Booth fled across the river by night after he had assassinated Lincoln.

Today the most celebrated highways through this region of the Potomac are not on the rivers, or even through the Great Valley, but along the Blue Ridge. Seeing the Ridge at a distance one may easily confuse the earthy with the ethereal: Where does the enveloping blue haze coalesce with rock? Where does the cliff wreathe and trail off into vapor? But the apparition not only has substance, it pulsates with the life of wild plants and animals. Thanks to the foresight of various men earlier in this century, much of the Blue Ridge and its life are preserved in a great national park. For access the ridge is traversed by two remarkable but very different highways, the Appalachian Trail and the Skyline Drive.

During the 1920s Benton MacKaye, an author and planner, promoted the idea of a trail that would extend as a wilderness cord through the eastern mountains from Georgia to Maine. The idea of an "Appalachian Trail" for hikers was taken up by other wilderness enthusiasts and became a reality. The Virginia section of the trail follows remnants of old Indian paths along the Blue Ridge and crosses the Potomac at Harpers Ferry. In breadth of view and in closeness to the plants and animals of the forest, the trail provides the adventurous hiker with one of the most rewarding experiences to be found in the Potomac watershed. MacKaye appreciated the value of such an experience. "Of several walkers 'doing' the Trail," he once said, "I'd give the prize to the slowest."

Even before the Appalachian Trail penetrated the Blue Ridge, popular summer resorts had sprung up there among the forests of chestnut oak and other hardwoods. The most famous was Skyland, built by George Freeman Pollock at Stony Man Mountain above Luray. Pollock, an expansive host and consummate showman, attracted thousands of vacationists and sportsmen, as well as Presidents and leaders of industry, to his resort. (Herbert Hoover was a great fancier of the area.) Pollock liked to put on entertaining shows around the tents and cabins of his resort in the evenings, live rattlesnakes and flamboyant Indians competing by firelight with ghost stories. But even more, he liked to believe that the surrounding forests would survive him, an unlikely possibility at the time because of the loggers' plans and the attendant threats of fire.

Eventually Pollock and his influential friends, Senator Harry F. Byrd among them, devised a plan to create a great eastern national park on the Blue Ridge. The Virginia legislature appropriated money to buy private holdings in the area. During the Depression thousands of adults and children contributed their dollars and pennies to swell the fund. On the eve of the Fourth of July in 1936, President Franklin D. Roosevelt dedicated the new park, three hundred square miles of forests at elevations up to four thousand feet, for the "recreation and re-creation which we shall find here." It was called Shenandoah for the river that winds through the valley below, surely the loveliest name bestowed on any of our national parks.

On that long-ago day Roosevelt and his party set off on a ride "through the clouds" on the first section of the Skyline Drive. This conception of a mountain highway, though not appropriate for some of the wilder national parks, was a happy one at Shenandoah. The drive twists along the Blue Ridge for 105 miles, giving motorists breathtaking views of the mountains themselves, worn down by time, the bare bones of the old earth clothed in season by flowering dogwoods and redbuds, gentle forest greens, and the fiery outbursts of autumn; in winter the drive is often closed because of fog, snow, and ice. The many parking overlooks afford other views across the checkered fabric of the valley floor.

Despite the occasional excesses of industrialization, these interior provinces of the Potomac Valley remain among the loveliest parts of America. The farms and estates of the piedmont and the valleys, the homesteads scattered along the ridges, and the wild things that still inhabit the hardwood forests make a visit there a delight at any time of the year. The Blue Ridge is especially rich in history. But what one visitor to the ridge in spring remembers best is the Catoctin greenstone breaking down to a reddish soil, while bloodroots, hepaticas, anenomes, and spring beauties bloomed there just as they did for those emigrants from the tidewater country two hundred years before.

At Harpers Ferry, West Virginia, the Potomac is swelled by its largest tributary, the Shenandoah River, which flows from the southwest along the floor of the Great Valley. A toll bridge spanned the river until it was swept away by floodwaters in 1936. A record crest over thirty-six feet above flood stage also destroyed the lower section of the historic town.

In Shenandoah National Park wildlife has been protected since the park was dedicated in 1936. Today, black bears and bobcats are occasionally found along the Skyline Drive, and the Virginia whitetailed deer is almost certain to be seen. This late summer's fawn, born a few months earlier, will soon lose its spots and assume the somber hues of the winter coat.

Loveliest of all June blossoms is the purple flowering raspberry. Not abundant, it grows by woodland edges along the Skyline Drive. In early autumn, it produces a bright red berry about the size of a quarter and shaped like a cloth-covered button.

The special brilliance of the fall colors on Stony Man Mountain in Shenandoah National Park is due largely to the mountain ash. Bright yellows, reds, and oranges of this dweller of the peaks add to the more subtle shades of the oaks and hickories to bring a showy climax to the season.

Rich mosses and pure waters characterize the Rapidan River, Herbert Hoover's trout stream, in Shenandoah National Park. Below this point is Hoover Camp, where the President found escape from the problems of the Depression years.

Large-flowered trilliums cover the hillsides in Shenandoah National Park in early May. White at first, they turn a delicate pink with age, but in soils with an abundance of iron they are pink from the start.

Forecasting midsummer's luscious wild feasts, blackberries bloom in late May and June at Big Meadows, Shenandoah National Park.

Cutting the Skyline Drive was a major engineering task, and for many years the raw scars were out of consonance with the natural surroundings. But today the bared stone has weathered to mellow red-browns and blue-grays to provide a rich background for a native rock garden.

Large stands of the wild spiraea, or meadowsweet, cover the wet places in Shenandoah National Park. The spiked clusters of flowers seem especially attractive to the smaller insects. This stand in Big Meadows blooms in July.

The shapes of nature are infinite in their variety. At Hemlock Springs Overlook, a gnarled oak unfolds its leaves in the early morning sun.

From the Skyline Drive, the morning sun shines through the spring foliage and accentuates the shapes of the Blue Ridge Mountains.

Foliose lichens thrive in the wetness of the high places in Shenandoah National Park.

The Northern Neck, granted in 1688 by James II to Lord Culpeper, included all the land between the Potomac and Rappahannock rivers. Subsequent surveys run by Lord Fairfax, heir to the grant, fixed the headwaters of the Rappahannock at the source of the Rapidan River near the Skyline Drive.

Filtered through the trees, sunlight dapples a waterfall on a tributary of Naked Creek in Shenandoah National Park.

PART V

HEADWATERS

A river's nature depends on where it begins, how it grows, and what its surroundings are. It is really the sum of what happens—now and in the past—in its watershed, or natural basin. The rain falling into that basin trickles and filters in the direction in which the land is tilted. It gathers in small streams which grow in size as they meet other swollen rivulets flowing down the basin's slopes. Finally these streams—and the soil and filth that have washed into them—come together to form a large river which is the basin's central "drain" and whose destination is the sea.

The Potomac has its official source in the Allegheny Highlands. There, at a point marked by the Fairfax Stone (which since 1910 has also served as the baseline for the western boundary of Maryland), lies that "first fountain of the Potowmack" mentioned in the royal charter granted to Lord Fairfax. This "source" is somewhat at variance with the geographic facts. It is based, first of all, on a royal grant that was eventually inherited by Thomas, the sixth Lord Fairfax, and that included most of the Northern Neck that lies between the Potomac and the Rappahannock. In determining the northwest corner of his huge estate in 1746, the surveyors employed by Lord Fairfax established this point as the Potomac's source. It *is* the source of one of the Potomac's arms, the North Branch, but later challengers to the validity of the Fairfax boundary (among them the Commonwealth of Virginia, Lord Baltimore of Maryland, and finally the new state of West Virginia) made the claim with much logic that the surveyors should have selected the source of the Potomac's South Branch instead, since it is longer and begins farther to the west than its northern counterpart. But the United States Supreme Court ruled in favor of the original decision in 1910.

In any event, enterprising tourists in West Virginia today may actually stand on the controversial spot. To reach it one must drive along mountain roads past slag heaps from extinct strip mines, now partly disguised under a stubble of recently planted red pines. Drainage from these and other mines has seeped into the underlying water here, so that the Potomac actually starts out its life as a polluted rivulet. One comes upon a plaque, set in a stone that has replaced an earlier one apparently spirited away by vandals. The plaque reads:

THIS MONUMENT, AT THE HEADSPRING OF THE POTOMAC RIVER, MARKS ONE OF THE HISTORIC SPOTS OF AMERICA. ITS NAME IS DERIVED FROM THOMAS LORD FAIRFAX WHO OWNED ALL THE LAND LYING BETWEEN THE POTOMAC AND RAPPAHANNOCK RIVERS. THE FIRST FAIRFAX STONE MARKED "FX" WAS SET IN 1746 BY THOMAS LEWIS, A SURVEYOR EMPLOYED BY LORD FAIRFAX. THIS IS THE BASE POINT FOR THE DIVIDING LINE BETWEEN MARYLAND AND WEST VIRGINIA.

Below the stone lies a leaf-clogged puddle in a small depression. The puddle releases a trickle that winds through a clump of scraggly beeches, utters its first sound as it drops into a shallow pool, and then sets off under a rail fence into the woods on its journey to the sea.

Whether or not this marker actually identifies the source, it is just such water on the move that creates the Potomac River Basin. The shape of the nearly fifteen thousand square miles drained by the Potomac has been compared to that of a boomerang. The two main branches flow in a northeasterly direction, the North Branch forming the border between Maryland and West Virginia, the South Branch and its chief tributaries nosing erratically through West Virginia as they probe for gaps and soft spots in some of the oldest rocks on earth. Below Cumberland, Maryland, they join to form the Potomac itself and turn sharply back to the southeast, flowing toward the piedmont plateau and the tidewater country and finally emptying into Chesapeake Bay.

The Allegheny Plateau where the Potomac begins is a part of the great Appalachian Mountain chain that rises in Alabama and Georgia and extends through eastern North America to the Gaspé Peninsula. There the mountains plunge into the Gulf of St. Lawrence, their peaks reappearing sporadically as islands and finally expiring as low ridges on the western shore of Newfoundland.

The plateau is the first of the major geologic regions through which the Potomac flows on its 383-mile journey. Bison used to roam the Allegheny valleys, their only traces now a few place-names such as Buffalo Hill and Buffalo Run (reminders that man often bestows names on his localities not as descriptions but as memorials). The last bison were killed in West Virginia's Randolph County in 1825. Elk survived into the 1870s, and wolves, despite man's neurotic hatred and official bounties, hung on until about 1900. Deer and beavers, practically extirpated also at one time, have made heartening comebacks. In the deer's case, at least, their numbers are probably greater today than they were when the first settlers reached the mountains.

It is in this region that many of the Potomac's twenty major tributaries empty into it. For the most part they are the youthful, fast-moving streams

of mountain country, rippling and foaming through V-shaped troughs they
have cut for themselves in the rocks on their rush to join the mother river. The water is always cool and sometimes clear. There are fine canoeing streams in the mountains where glistening white puffs of spray warn canoeists away from rocks in the stream bed.

An experienced observer can tell a great deal about the bottom composition just from noting the speed of the stream's flow. One doesn't have to peer at the bottom to know what kind of sand or gravel will be found there, or what mosses, algae, and invertebrate organisms. Here, as in swiftly moving streams anywhere in the world, one will find insects and other minute invertebrates living behind and under the stones, their eggs provided with sticky substances that keep them clinging to handy surfaces even in the face of the torrent. Stone-fly larvae slip into cracks between stones and hold themselves in place with their tenacious claws. Nearby are clusters of caddis-fly larvae, encased in their neat cylinders of grains and pebbles. Small birds such as the Louisiana water thrush patrol the shores, looking for insects. But the king of this environment is the trout, lurking in those turbulent riffles near stones where it finds the stone flies and other aquatic insects on which it lives.

Spring in the Potomac highlands is a joy not only for the trout fisherman and the adventurous canoeist in the surging rivers but also for the casual observer. Visit the West Virginia mountains on one of those changeable days that add to the excitement and expectancy of early spring. You drive through a succession of ridges and valleys at the edge of the Allegheny Plateau. The road carries you through small towns (there is one in its narrow valley named Onego, pronounced locally as "won-go") and past isolated farms. The floors of the high valleys, as if not subject to gravity, keep erupting in rounded nubbles. Often the only level lines in view are the shallow terraces worn across the steeply tilted fields by cattle as they graze the brownish-green grass that has not yet taken on the emerald tint of spring; perhaps there is a sound basis for the old tall tales about cows falling out of Allegheny pastures. Where water seeps downhill just beneath the surface, the fields are streaked with dark green rills.

At the town of Mouth of Seneca a monolithic fist of quartzite thrusts itself a thousand feet above the rushing water and leaning sycamores near the mouth of Seneca Creek. These Seneca Rocks, said by climbers to be the best rock climb in the East (and dubbed by promotion men "the Face of One Thousand Pitons"), are a part of the magnificent Monongahela National Forest. Here the creek enters the North Fork of the South Branch of the Potomac River. Here is the heart of the Potomac highlands.

In the rocky flow of Seneca Creek, which runs northeast from its source on Spruce Mountain, fishermen stand and angle for rainbow trout, for this is one of the few streams in the region where the rainbows reproduce themselves and do not have to be restocked by the state in an endless round of put-and-take. A spreading translucence of sky makes known the sun's presence somewhere above the dominant gray cloud mass. The forest mounts the steep slopes on both sides of the stream. Beneath the budding trees shine a surf of wildflowers, dazzling in their color and variety. There are spring beauties, bloodroots, red trilliums, hepaticas, yellow violets, chickweeds, may-apples (just poking through the debris on the forest floor, like tightly wrapped little green umbrellas), and, among the rocks, the pretty white blossoms of early saxifrage.

At last the leaden sky crumbles beneath its burden of light, and sun shafts fall through to glint and burst on the buoyant creek. If you leave your car and walk upstream under the warm sun, you will pass many small and noisy waterfalls along the way. On most such days your attention is likely to be caught by dozens of bent figures moving singly or in groups slowly up the hillsides under the forest canopy. There are men, women, and children. They dig with trowels and even small shovels in the dark earth and its low herbage. From a distance it looks as if the diggers are filling boxes and other containers with the leaves and stems of wild lilies such as Clintonia.

But in answer to the visitor's natural question, a small boy looks up and utters a single word in a rolling twang: "Ramps."

Ramps. Then these people are rampers, digging the wild leek (*Allium tricoccum*) for home consumption or for sale to restaurants and the promoters of various "ramp festivals" throughout West Virginia where tourists and the local people assemble to eat ramps with ham, corn bread, and other regional delicacies. These plants, with long, lilylike leaves and reddish stems, are prized for their bulbs, which contain a potent essence of garlic. Although they bear no relation to rampion, that Eurasian vegetable for which Rapunzel's mother acquired such a fateful craving, they are not soon forgotten by anyone who bites into them. As the West Virginia naturalist Maurice Brooks has written, "Even the rabid ramp-eater will admit, if pressed, that he grows a little tired of the taste about three days after he has feasted."

Here, in the mountains where the Potomac has its origin, there are boundless treasures, animal, vegetable, and mineral. The mountains are very old and were originally formed by the tilting and folding of sedimentary rocks, then eroded and leveled through millions of years to their present maximum height of around four thousand feet. There is a kind of limited "continental divide" here. Some of the rivulets on the Allegheny Plateau eventually gather in streams and rivers pointed westward toward the Ohio River, and then into the Mississippi and the Gulf of Mexico, while others rush north and eastward into the Potomac and finally to Chesapeake Bay and the Atlantic Ocean.

The flora of these mountains is northern, contrasting with the more southerly plants found in lowlands at the same latitudes. Thus plants one expects to find in Maine or New Brunswick also thrive on the chilled, wind-swept ridges of the Potomac highlands. Yet the glaciers that covered so much of the northern United States did not reach into what is now West Virginia. These mountains during the glaciation provided a sanctuary for many northern plants that otherwise would have become extinct under thousands of feet of ice. When the glaciers receded, the plants that survived in this region crept north again in their wake. It is an interesting phenomenon that many of the species found in these mountains (trillium, trailing arbutus, Jack-in-the-pulpit, skunk cabbage, dwarf ginseng) have close relations in China or Japan where similar north-south running mountain chains did not permit the flora to be "trapped." In much of Eurasia to the west of China the mountains (such as the Himalayas, the Alps, and the Pyrenees) run east and west, and there was no route of preservation on which northern plants could escape southward along a line of ridges beyond reach of the glaciers' white tentacles. The flora of northern Europe, for instance, is meager in comparison to that of the United States.

And so the mountain people have found more than ramps around them. Of greater value and with a longer tradition for these people is ginseng, that herb which the Chinese brought to the world's attention as a panacea. Not the least of ginseng's virtues, according to the Chinese, is the utility of its forked root as an aphrodisiac. The true ginseng (*Panax schinseng*) is native to eastern Asia. But the Chinese found no dimunition of virtue in the closely related American ginseng (*Panax quinquefolius*), and for many years (until they pushed it to the edge of extinction) the mountain people enjoyed a good income by collecting "sang" for export. The tidewater people may firmly believe in the potency of their oysters, but apparently ginseng's chief use in China was not fully appreciated by the American "sangers." They knew only that it was a "medicine." Because ginseng's cluster of small greenish flowers is inconspicuous, it is collected most easily in the fall when its bright red berries mature. Donald Culross Peattie once heard a mountain man describe the "sangers":

> They was the most terrifying people I ever see. I was over in the balsams near the pink beds, when I see them coming through the woods —men and women with eyes that didn't seem to see nothing, and their

clothes all in tatters, and their hair all lank and falling down on their shoulders. They humped along through the woods like b'ars, muttering to themselves all the time, and stooping and digging, and cursing and humping on and digging again.

The mountains have provided other wild things in quantity, including game, for the people who settled there. Perhaps the most famous hunter of the region was Meshack Browning. A man of action, as old Meshack was, often confirms his reputation by writing a book about himself. Browning's book, *Forty-Four Years of a Hunter*, published in 1859, enjoyed considerable popularity and stirred up some skepticism. In describing his years of glory in the field (1795–1839), he told of killing two thousand deer, five hundred bears (many of them in their winter dens, which he invaded by candlelight), fifty panthers, and a variety of other big game. Browning was a skilled marksman with the long rifle, and a wily tracker and woodsman. Here is his description of bear hunting:

> I always kept two good dogs; one of which walked before me, and the other behind. The one in front would wind the bear, and lead me up to him on that side on which he could not smell me, for I would come on him unexpectedly. If, by chance, he found us coming on him, and ran, the dogs would overtake him before he would be out of sight. The moment I would see one run, I would send the dogs after him; and as I could run almost as fast as any bear could, when the fight began I was close up, and a shot was certain death. In many cases, however, I killed them with my knife; but only when the fight was so close that I was afraid to shoot lest I should kill a dog; which has often been done. I never in my life shot a dog in a fight; for I always took a knife in a close contest.

The wealth of big game had nearly dried up by the time of Browning's death in 1859. Browning himself attributed much of the decline to cattle, turned out to pasture all over the mountains and overgrazing the land which once had sustained the wild creatures of the region. Certainly that and the ruthless felling of the forests for timber played their part in the disappearance of big game. But just as certainly the indiscriminate shooting finished off animal populations already sorely depleted by their dwindling habitat. Wild turkeys, particularly tame and "stupid" in those early days, were nearly eliminated from the mountains. John James Audubon, traveling west through Cumberland in 1843, wrote that he and his party "saw much game on our way, such as geese, ducks, etc., but no turkeys as in times of yore." In our own time these large birds, fortified by a new wariness of man, are increasing.

Their sudden gobble, or their persistent scratching among the dry leaves, may be heard often in the woods today, and drivers are likely to see them along certain roads early in the morning, apparently picking up grit to aid in digesting their food.

Occasionally one hears a report that someone has sighted a panther (or mountain lion) in the West Virginia mountains. The report is generally discounted by naturalists. Like wolves, panthers carried a bounty on their heads, and the bounty hunters pursued them relentlessly. The panther has almost certainly been exterminated in the region. People who caught glimpses of ghostly panthers in the recent past are now more likely, under the present inducements of media coverage, to detect flying saucers.

Man has altered not only the composition of the mountain fauna; he has altered the face of the land too. For a while the primitive frontier civilization could make no lasting scar on this pristine face, though the forests were cut for fuel, building materials, and tanbark, and coal hacked by itinerant miners from seams was shipped on flatboats down the Potomac.

But the railroad intensified man's pressure on the land. It was soon apparent that in this region lay one of the world's richest deposits of coal, and after the tracks reached Cumberland in 1842, there seemed no limit on the amount of coal that could be shipped cheaply out of the mountains.

The Civil War (or "the War Amongst Us," as the mountain people called it) had its impact on the region too. The mountains served as an important battleground where rival armies fought for control of the railroad and the water gaps that were the main lines of communication between East and West. The people of western Virginia largely remained loyal to the Union, a stance that caused their area to be torn from the staunchly Confederate commonwealth of Virginia and established as a state in its own right. After the war, mostly ignored by their Southern country cousins in the lowlands, the mountain people lapsed into isolation. Powerful trusts such as the Consolidation Coal Company, financed in New York and Boston and controlling regional railroads, extracted the coal and timber and shipped these resources to other areas of the country. They left behind a scarred land, polluted streams, and a pauperized people.

From the lowlands today, these mountains present a uniform front, adamantine, featureless. But on close inspection they are seen to be honeycombed by a wealth of exuberant natural communities. They remain a garden of delights for the curious naturalist. The streams of the Potomac highlands often drop precipitously in silver curtains, shifting from one level to another. The open rocky slopes are glazed by sun and phlox. There are the unique shale barrens scattered through the mountains, with hoary puccoon, prickly pear, and other wildflowers growing out of the eroded red earth, and the weathered slate flaking off the hillsides as the tips of a bird's feathers break away under constant wear.

Place names conjure up hours of delightful exploration. There are the Dolly Sods (named after a German pioneer family, the Dahles, whose livestock grazed on the open grassy areas called "sods" in these mountains), set high over the North Fork of the South Branch; birders gather there in the fall for unobstructed views of the waves of migrating hawks.

There is West Virginia's Spruce Knob, at 4,862 feet the highest point in the Potomac watershed (and indeed, from Pine Mountain in southern Virginia to Mount Marcy, New York, where the Hudson River has its source, there is none higher). Its lofty, inhospitable shoulders are often called "the land of the one-sided trees." Plagued by fierce winds and rocky soils, even red spruces more than a half century old seldom attain a height of fifteen feet, and they are generally stripped of their branches on all but the southeastern side. From Spruce Knob's observation tower (easily reached by car) the Potomac highlands east and west are served up nearly intact for one's fascinated regard.

There is the lush Canaan Valley (pronounced "kah-*nane*") tucked in the mountains, with its pretty state park providing a site for numbers of beaver houses and dams.

There is Smoke Hole Canyon, where the Potomac's South Branch has carved various caves and spectacular formations out of the limestone. Perhaps the most wonderful is Smoke Hole Cave, its dim central chamber tapering to a natural chimney where Indians and later the early white settlers "smoke cured" their meats. Small brown bats cling to the damp walls here, while outside the purple-stemmed cliff brake droops in feathery profusion on the ledges.

There are the "blister swamps," an Appalachian name for wetlands, where balsam firs (or "blister pines"), their trunks studded with blisterlike seepages of resin, approach the southern limit of their range. Within them one breathes the aroma of the north woods. Around them the open air above the wet meadows is harsh with the alarm calls of snipe, flushed from the tall grass by farmers or hikers.

Few places in these mountains harbor such exotic diversity as the bogs, wet areas of sphagnum moss, often with layers of sedge peat and algal ooze below, locally called "glades." Perhaps the most fascinating of these is Cranberry Glades in the Monongahela National Forest. Glades are akin to a northern muskeg in their plants and animals. The alert visitor may see orchids such as *Calapogon* and rose pogonia, and insectivorous plants such as sundew, horned bladderwort, and pitcher plant (the latter transplanted to Cranberry Glades from a Pennsylvania bog!). He may hear hermit thrushes and mourning warblers.

Fortunately, Cranberry Glades is now preserved within the Monongahela National Forest as a Botanical Area. For too long the notion has persisted that bogs, swamps, marshes, and other wetlands are, at best, "waste places" and, at worst, reservoirs of evil spirits and loathly creatures, to be entered at one's peril, like Conan Doyle's great Grimpen Mire. Such notions have made it easy for the exploiters to deprive the Potomac Valley, by filling in the salt marshes of the tidewater country as well as the highland bogs, of much of its diversity.

Today the mountains themselves are threatened by man and his earth-moving machines. Entrepreneurs of many stripes have concocted plans to dam the Cheat River, flood the Canaan Valley, strip the coal from the Cranberry backcountry, and stipple the grandest peaks with leisure homes. Promoters, strippers, and highway builders infest the remotest hills and valleys. Natural beauty is grist for their dingy mills.

But until now the mountains in their mass have survived the worst of our schemes. They rise, bristling ridge on ridge, sundered, sometimes it seems, from the earth itself, but piled among the clouds, the ripe clouds grounding out on the ridges as ships on a ledge, their burden of rain ripped from their keels, and then sailing on in streaming tatters. It is comforting to hope that man's destructive ingenuity, too, will come to grief on those static explosions of ancient rock. The impulse that sent them bursting through the earth's shell has faltered, but their splendors endure. Not the least of those splendors is the river that the mountains nurture in a thousand rills and brooks and send on its timeless way past the seedbed of our nation's history to the distant sea.

This small stream, the North Fork of the South Branch, is thought by many to mark the true headwaters of the Potomac River. Had the surveyors of the Northern Neck grant chosen this source, the grant would have contained much more land, and the course of history in the Potomac Valley would have followed different lines.

Surrounded by stone to protect its historic value, a trickle of spring water emerges from the ancient Appalachian rocks. Here at an elevation of 3,150 feet (near Thomas, West Virginia), the Potomac begins its journey to the sea. Three hundred eighty-three miles farther and seven miles wider, it enters Chesapeake Bay at Point Lookout.

From the highlands through the piedmont, the Potomac slips over rock-covered valleys. Year after year, the waters dissolve the binding elements or wear away the stone grain by grain. Always seeking the path of least resistance, the waters slide around the harder rocks and erode those that are less durable. Tomorrow the river may find a new course and these rocks, now covered, will stand on a bluff above the river. This is the South Branch, near Upper Tract, West Virginia.

In a springtime pasture near Smoke Hole, the nearly full-grown leaves of maples show a golden green that is too soon lost.

August brings the subdued lavender-pink hues of hollow Joe-Pye weed to roadsides and open places along the Potomac and other streams. Four species of Joe-Pye weed bloom along the river from tidewater to the headsprings.

A solitary stone chimney is all that remains of this mountain home high above the Potomac near Petersburg, West Virginia. Ravaged by fire, consumed by wood-eating insects, or dry-rotted, the wooden parts disappear first, completing nature's recycling plan. Left alone, the chimney may stand for two or three generations before it too succumbs to the forces of wind, water, and ice. Then, in a tumbled heap, the aged rocks will last another eon till even they will be gone.

A hand-carved stone and some plastic flowers memorialize those buried in a family plot on North Fork Mountain near Franklin, West Virginia. The shale chips mounded over the graves tell of the hard life the mountaineers must have known. Now the farm is abandoned and cattle graze in the front yard of the house.

*Tinged by tannin leached from the northern bog forest of the Canaan Valley,
the Blackwater River makes a spectacular descent through a deep gorge.
The headspring of the Blackwater's North Fork lies half a mile from the
headspring of the Potomac at the Fairfax Stone. Yet their courses are totally
different, for the eastern continental divide follows a ridge between them. Via
the Blackwater, Cheat, Monongahela, Ohio, and Mississippi, these cold
mountain waters will journey thousands of miles to the warm Gulf of Mexico.*

Like a flaming torch, a young red maple seems to shout its defiance as it clings to a precarious foothold on the rocks in the river. The brilliant reds and oranges of fall colors are produced by the hydrocarbon compound carotene. This is the Blackwater River near Davis, West Virginia.

The south branch of the Potomac River is a three-tined fork above Moorefield, West Virginia. All three forks have their origins across the state line in Highland County, Virginia. The middle tine, known simply as the South Branch River, flows a parallel course separated from the other two by North Fork Mountain and South Fork Mountain. Below Moorefield the river widens and slows as it passes Romney and joins the North Branch east of Green Spring, West Virginia, and Oldtown, Maryland.

The Dolly Sods present a severe challenge to trees. Higher than the mountains to the north-west, the Sods sit broadside to the prevailing winds. Unimpeded the gales sweep down upon the boulder-strewn plains as if to tear away all living things. In winter, ice storms load the trees and break their limbs. Stunted by the rigorous forces, aspens assume grotesquely beautiful shapes and bend with the wind and survive. But the tough, wiry shrubs of the heath family are the kings of this environment. Growing close to the ground, huckleberries and laurels are the hardiest of plants and thrive where others fail.

The maples color the seasons along the Potomac. In the tidewater plains at the end of a mild winter, the inconspicuous blossoms tinge the twigs maroon. In May the winged seeds have former, bringing a russet orange or brighter red. Summer's rich greens cool the hotter days, and in October the maples light the mountains with nearly every shade of the spectrum from green through yellow to brilliant red.

Too small for trout, the many rivulets that course through mountain ravines nevertheless add to the abundant wildlife that thrives in pure-water habitats. Salamanders are plentiful along such streams. Myriads of insects spend their larval stages in these small rills. And the state of West Virginia boasts fifteen different kinds of crayfish including a rarely seen indigo-blue species, Cambarus monongalensis.

A cricket blends into the rich colors and shapes of patterned lichens on a rock at Spruce Knob. In some rocky, exposed locations lichens are the only living plants.

Late June brings the flowering of the mountain
laurel to the Potomac highlands. At Dolly Sods
National Wilderness Area, near Petersburg, West
Virginia, hundreds of acres are spread with the
pink bloom in what surely is this shrub's finest
display in America. Its name is a misnomer, for
"mountain" laurel enriches the tidewater scene,
growing as it does at sea level. Indeed, it is found
at all levels, wherever the Potomac flows.

The late-afternoon sun highlights the ridges and
shades the ravines of North Fork Mountain. For
millions of years, nature has carved these shapes with
water. Each ravine has its rivulet rushing down the
mountain. The rivulets join to form creeks, reinforced
as they go by spring waters seeping laterally along the
mountainside. Two thousand feet below, the accumulated flow joins the North Fork.

The faster water runs, the less likely it is to freeze. Near rocks in a stream, the waters eddy and lose speed, making it easier for ice crystals to form. Droplets of spray are deposited on the rocks, where they freeze within seconds. With ice formed around the edges of the rocks, new ice forms more readily. As growth rings tell the age of a tree, ice rings around a rock mark the changing levels of the stream. At the very edge, lacy fringes of another ring are formed by tiny icicles extending down to the new level. This is Red Creek, near Laneville, West Virginia.

At elevations above four thousand feet, the Dolly Sods National Wilderness Area consists of an immense boulder field, stunted evergreens, and other small trees and shrubs. In fall, the yellow birches give their golden blessing to the mountain.

As though in a witch's forest, the candelabralike roots of a fallen spruce rise above the black ripples of a mountain pond in Canaan Valley State Park, near Davis, West Virginia. Red spruce grows at the higher elevations in the Allegheny Mountains and used to be an important source of lumber. But once cut, the boreal spruce forests do not return naturally until the end of a long successional chain. When this happens, the entire biotic order of the northern spruce forest is disturbed, and the northern warblers, thrushes, and other species disappear. In the distant future the spruces will come back when the forest provides them with protection from the fierce winds of the high places.

The beaver, nature's engineer, has an instinct for ecology. Wherever his dams go up, a new habitat forms which fits the needs of the many species that will soon occupy it. Over the ages, the slow, sure process of natural selection has fitted wildlife and beaver pond to each other, and now it is a time-tested environment. Brook trout thrive on the many insects and crustaceans that breed in the pond. Wood ducks dabble for food and fledge their young from the hollows of dead trees. Orchids and gentians bloom in the wet meadows. The valley is never destroyed . . . only enriched.

Like waves in an earthen sea, the mountains roll ridge on ridge to the dim horizon. The table mountain pine, an uncommon tree of the higher peaks, grows here on Kyle Knob near Franklin, West Virginia, amid the brilliant reds of November huckleberries.

The Indians called the South Branch the Wappatomaka. To them it was a different river, tributary to the Potomac. The early settlers may have been confused by the similarity of the two names. Whatever the reason, Wappatomaka lost its identity as a river. The upper reaches of the Potomac were called the North Branch and the Wappatomaka became the South Branch.

On rare occasions nature brings together the right conditions of climate, geology, and botany to produce a garden of surpassing beauty. Such a place is Cranberry Glades in West Virginia's Monongahela National Forest. Known for their rare plants and delicate orchids, the glades are reserved for scientific study. Here they take on special beauty as autumn forests tinge the grasses and enrich the graceful cinnamon ferns.

SELECTED READING

Briggs, Shirley A. (editor). *The Potomac Valley: History and Prospect.* Washington, D.C.: Audubon Society of the District of Columbia, 1952.

Brooks, Maurice G. *The Appalachians.* Boston: Houghton Mifflin Company, 1965.

Brown, Stuart E., Jr. *Annals of Blackwater and the Land of Canaan.* Berryville, Va.: Chesapeake Book Company, 1959.

Burroughs, John. *Wake Robin.* Boston: Houghton Mifflin Company, 1885.

Coues, Elliott, and D. Webster Prentiss. *Avifauna Columbiana.* U.S. National Museum Bulletin No. 26. Washington, D.C.: U.S. Government Printing Office, 1883.

Cutright, Paul R. *Theodore Roosevelt the Naturalist.* New York: Harper & Brothers, 1956.

Gutheim, Frederick A. *The Potomac.* New York: Rinehart & Company, 1949.

Halle, Louis J. *Spring in Washington.* New York: William Sloane Associates, 1947.

Maynard, Mrs. L. W. *Birds of Washington and Vicinity.* Washington, D.C.: n.p., 1902.

Morrison, Charles. *The Fairfax Line: A Profile in History and Geography.* Parsons, W.Va.: McClain Printing Company, 1970.

———. *Wappatomaka: A Survey of the History and Geography of the South Branch Valley.* Parsons, W.Va.: McClain Printing Company, 1971.

Pogue, Robert E. T. *Old Maryland Landmarks.* Bushwood, Md.: n.p., 1972.

Posey, Calvert R. *An Ecological History of Charles County, Maryland.* La Plata, Md.: The Times-Crescent, 1971.

Sanderlin, Walter. *The Great National Project: A History of the Chesapeake and Ohio Canal.* Baltimore: Johns Hopkins Press, 1946.

Shosteck, Robert. *Potomac Trail Book.* Washington, D.C.: Potomac Books, 1973.

Smith, J. Lawrence. *Blackwater Country.* Parsons, W.Va.: McClain Printing Company, 1972.

———. *The Potomac Naturalist.* Parsons, W.Va.: McClain Printing Company, 1968.

Strother, David Hunter. "The Virginian Canaan." *Harper's New Monthly Magazine,* VIII, 18–36 (Dec. 1853). Reprinted in *Georgia Review,* XIX, No. I, 94–120 (1965).

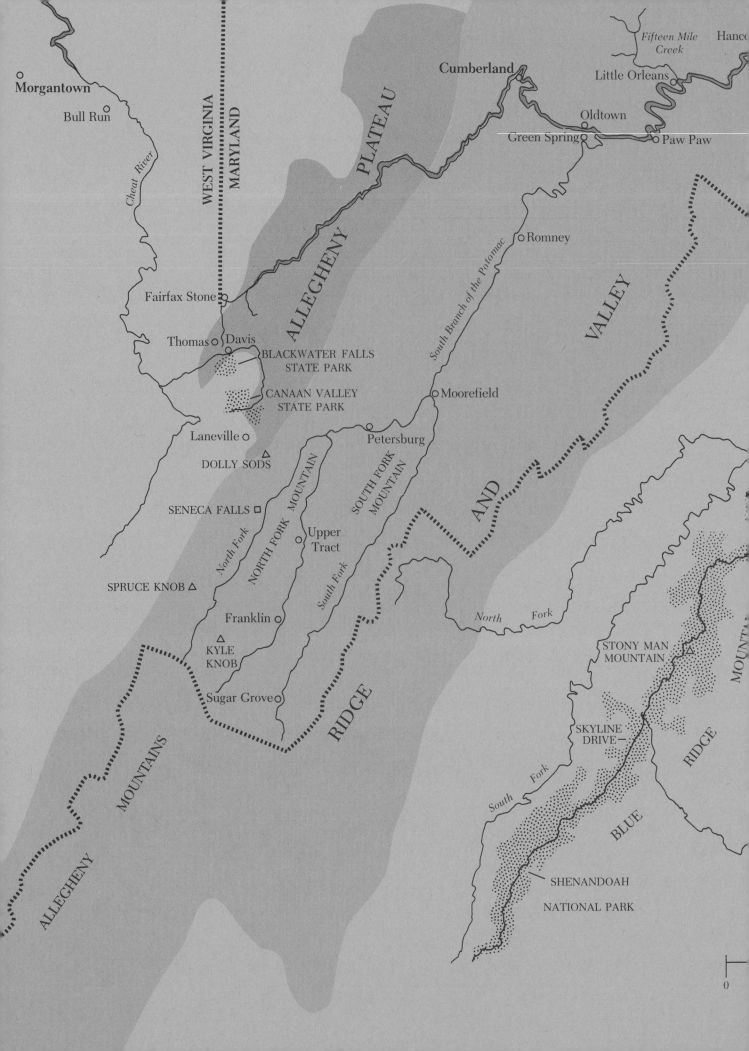